High
on
Being

High on Being

A trail guide to Living Fully Alive.

MICHAEL J. GRIMES

Published by Author Academy Elite
PO Box 43, Powell, OH 43065
www.AuthorAcademyElite.com

Identifiers:
LCCN: 2022907147
ISBN: 979-8-88583-064-5 (paperback)
ISBN: 979-8-88583-065-2 (hardback)
ISBN: 979-8-88583-066-9 (ebook)

Available in paperback, hardback, e-book.

This book is dedicated to everyone committed
to their personal journey.
It's dedicated to those who are doing their work
to learn from their past and live alive in the present.
It's for everyone who acknowledges
that the greatest gift we can give the world is our love and light.
It's dedicated to those who remember who they are and
who they're meant to be, and everyone showing up to life,
inspired and engaged.
This book is dedicated to the change agents,
critical thinkers, seekers, explorers, visionaries and light bearers.
Thank you for all you've done and all you will continue to do.
Together, we will bring forth a new world of love and light.
Thank you for all you've done to help us get to where we're at.
And thank you for all you will continue to do, to move us forward.
A new world is upon us.
We have you to thank.
Thank you for being you.
Thank you for being.

Table of Contents

<h1 style="text-align:center">Foreword
by Dan Miller</h1>

How easily we are identified by **what we do** rather than **who we are**. We live in a culture that embraces doing. It's a badge of honor to be "busy". We often talk about how busy we are with pride as if our exhaustion were a badge of honor and our ability to withstand the stress a mark of real character. The busier we are, the more important we seem to ourselves and possibly even others. Thus, we are often unavailable to those who need us, unable to enjoy a sunset, and deprived of personal balance. Solitude, meditation, or even thinking are not valued in modern America.

In *High on Being*, Michael supports us to optimize and maximize our earthly experience. As he promises, this book will "help you shift from living as a human doing to thriving as a human being."

Having spent three stays at The Abbey of Gethsemani, a monastery near Bardstown, KY, this issue is a poignant focus for me. The Abbey is a Trappist monastery where the expressed goal is "being", with that concept solidified by vows of chastity and poverty. As Michael shares in *High on Being*, many monks and spiritual practitioners remove the obstacles and struggles that most of us encounter rather than working to thrive within them. While there, I was free from TV, phones, social media, email, cars, Taco Bell and Pepsi. Although a voracious reader, I also did not allow myself any books, audio access, magazines, or newspapers. Removing these conveniences and pleasantries makes it much easier to connect with my higher self. The trick is in maintaining this connection while returning to the real world.

As much as I believe in physical breathing, I believe even more strongly that we need both symbolic inhaling and exhaling in our lives. If I only exhale physically, I will turn blue and pass out. If I am busy "doing", I will likely become exhausted and burn out. But I fear that if I inhale only ("being"), I will leave a void or vacuum around me. Rather than passing abundance and goodness on to others, I may appear to be self-absorbed and insensitive. We must embrace that sacred balance of rest and performance.

If I retreat and "do" nothing, I will miss my opportunity to fulfill my purpose and make a difference in the world. Aristotle said, "Where your greatest talents and the world's greatest needs cross, there lies your vocation."

We are told the difference between insanity and genius is success. In many things, there is a fine line between the desirable and the undesirable. In this example, I suspect that the line between *seeking spiritual wholeness* and *dropping out* is frequently indistinguishable. While at The Abbey, my room was adequate but sparse, having a desk, a chair, a lamp, and a cot. I happen to enjoy solitude and have never been a great socializer. However, the dropped eyes, the absence of the passing "Hi, how are you?" and the continued unconnectedness soon had even me longing for a little more interaction. How can having access to the earth's resources be displayed or utilized except through meaningful contact with the world and other people? How frustrating it would be to have a Ferrari in your garage but not have a key to the garage door. While there was a hypnotic reverence in the seven times daily choral chants, I began to feel I was trapped in Groundhog Day. I found myself sleeping more, simply in an attempt to make the hours pass more quickly.

If you are working 70 hours a week, you are probably trying to "do" too much. Give yourself a break to "be". After all, what we are **becoming** is always more important than what we are **achieving**. Spend time with your children, get a massage, light candles for the family dinner, hike through the park or visit a monastery.

In *High on Being*, Michael clarifies that while we have evolved to a place where we no longer need to *do* in order to survive, we still continue to base our life around *doing*. We must find the balance in the breath of *doing* and *being*. When we're *doing* what we love, it's beneficial *doing*. Moreso, *being* can even incorporate *doing* in our work when we find our "ikigia", the zone where our talents, passions, and societal needs meet. Finding that sweet spot will allow you to live out your highest value of *being* AND *doing*.

Most of us are looking for a more engaged, vibrant existence than living in a monastery. We savor the challenges and luxuries of life. We relish in the struggles and the beauties. We want to enjoy a glass of wine and have some passionate sex. Like Thoreau, we desire to "...live deliberately, to front only the essential facts of life, and see if I could not learn what it had to teach, and not, when I came to die, discover that I had not lived. I did not wish to live what was not life, living is so dear; nor did I wish to practice resignation, unless it was quite necessary. I wanted to live deep and suck out all the marrow of life, to live so sturdily and Spartan-like as to put to rout all that was not life, to cut a broad swath and shave close, to drive life into a corner, and reduce it to its lowest terms..."

This book is your guide for sucking all the marrow out of life. It gives you the zen bliss of the monastery with the realities of society to support you on the journey to living fully alive.

Introduction

Why are we here? Is there a reason for our existence? Where do we come from? And where do we go? These are foundational questions to the nature of existence we may never find definitive answers to. While gurus and religious texts answer these questions from their perspective, we must acknowledge that their answers are just that, their perspectives. Some beliefs might be more aligned with the universal consciousness and Truth than others, but it's hard to accept that any one answer can be entirely correct while the others are entirely wrong. It's hard to fathom that anyone has it all figured out.

Based on my experiences into the nature of existence -through a wide range of modalities- I've found that we've barely scratched the surface of understanding. We comprehend so little of what's going on around us, within us, and within the cosmos.

That being said, we're learning more every day as we continually evolve and grow as humanity. We probably know more today than we have at any point in time as we know it. We're figuring some things out. Our understanding of the human experience is deepening dramatically. Our connection to the spiritual realms grows stronger as the veil between realms is thinning. We're evolving. Rapidly.

And yet, we still know so little.

We may never truly know if there's a reason for our existence.

Yet, there are aspects of our existence we are finally starting to understand. We know that if you're reading this book right now, you're alive. Congratulations! You're blessed to be alive. We also know that life will bring challenges, and, at the same time, there's an opportunity to find beauty in all of it. We've found that our bodies hold the energy of past experiences and we need to integrate that energy of the past to be fully alive in the present. We're accepting the need to do self-work as we've found a variety of techniques to heal our mental and emotional bodies. We understand the benefits of yoga and meditation. We're embracing the benefits of plant based medicines. We're accepting that our thoughts help create our reality. We know that bliss accompanies love and that there are not many things more pleasurable than making love. And we know how fulfilling it can be to live a life you're passionate about.

This isn't to mention the scientific breakthroughs occurring daily or the ancient wisdom that's resurfacing.

We're living in a time of major expansion. We're evolving. Growing.

We're starting to embody our being and honor the life we've been blessed with. We're embracing the learnings we're presented with to maximize our earthly experience. We're living more fully alive. It's definitely not everyone. But it's many of us.

We're acknowledging there's more to life than working a 9-5 for 5 days a week so we can live on the weekend. We're seeing the benefits of doing the personal work necessary to integrate our past, find peace with our future, and live fully present in the eternal moment of now. We're finding that there's more to life than we can see with our eyes. We're accepting that it's not about what we do as much as it is who we are.

These are concrete shifts we're making to our understanding of the human experience.

I'm obsessed with these shifts.

I've been working to optimize and maximize my earthly experience for as long as I can remember. After my first awakening, I doubled down on this pursuit. I worked with spiritual masters, traveled solo, read the books, and picked the brains of those who were thriving. I leaned into doing the personal work while trying every modality I'm presented with that could support me to live more aligned with my true authentic self.

I'm blessed to have spent most of my life thriving, living fully alive.

But it hasn't always been easy. Some phases were straight-up hard. I've gone through my struggles. And yet, I've continued to emerge stronger, with greater perspective, insight, and wisdom. Each struggle has proved to be an opportunity for growth and expansion.

When I was in my early 20's, I went through a year of intense growth that cumulated with the suicide of my younger brother. It shattered my foundation. It felt like everything I thought and believed to be true was suddenly a lie. From this place, I was given the opportunity to rebuild my foundation stronger than it had previously been. This came at the end of a year in which I had full reconstructive knee surgery, wrote my college thesis, and found out that my girlfriend was messing around with my best friend.

I lost my physical abilities, my brain was fried, and my emotional and spiritual worlds were flipped upside down. This was my first extreme low. It was heavy and hard. And, from it, came my first awakening.

Fifteen years later, when I was pushed to walk away from the revolutionary charter school I served as co-founder and co-director, I was devastated. A year later, my wife moved out on the same day as my dad's funeral. Again, I hit an all-time low.

And again, I rebuilt with stronger pillars, allowing myself to expand further than before.

This is what we do as humans. We overcome obstacles to grow and evolve. We expand in a continual pursuit to experience ourselves more fully. Good, bad, and ugly. All of it. It's all part of who we are.

As we continue this cycle, we can support each other in overcoming these obstacles to evolve ourselves and reach new heights. Together, we can go farther than we can individually.

Personally, I've found some things that work. I've been through the valleys and stood on the mountain tops. And I've fallen from the summit to reclimb as an even greater version of myself.

My hope is that in sharing the best of what I've found, you can apply pieces to your journey. Granted, each journey is entirely individualized. You can apply strategies and techniques that have worked for me in your own way. There are common threads amongst our paths that allow us to learn from each other.

This book covers these common grounds. It addresses the areas we all walk. It encapsulates the big aspects of life while providing specific details, examples, and strategies for growth.

The book will help you shift from living as a human doing, to thriving as a human being. It combines ancient indigenous wisdom with modern mysticism, science, and understanding of the human condition, to help you align with your highest self and make the most of life.

It helps you further understand who you are and who you strive to be. *Being* supports you in questioning what you know and exploring your inner realms. It brings you back to these foundational aspects of self while exploring the leading edges of what's possible in human form.

And, while encouraging evolution and growth, *Being* reminds us that life is to be lived. Fully. With wonder, passion, awe, gratitude, excitement, fun, and love. It might take some work to get to this place, but it's the best kind of work we will ever do.

CHAPTER 1

Doing

We've become human doings.

"If we keep doing what we're doing, we're going to keep getting what we're getting."

-Stephen Covey, Author/Educator/Motivational Speaker

"Mindfulness means being awake. It means knowing what you are doing."

-Jon Kabat-Zinn, American Professor and creator of the Center for Mindfulness in Medicine, Health Care, and society

For the majority of human history, we've lived to survive. We've lived to continue living. Everything else was secondary.

We needed food, water, shelter, and sleep. And we needed to reproduce. In return, our time was spent obtaining these needs. We hunted and gathered, collected and carried water, built shelter, and slept.

Once we met these needs, we got to be.

We lived freely in nature and connected with the land and our tribe. After work was complete, we were free. We made music that we danced and sang along to. We conversed around the fire, sharing experiences, reflections, ideas, and beliefs. We'd gaze upon the stars in wonder and awe. We'd think, talk, and dream.

But during the day, we worked to survive. We did our best to meet our basic human needs while keeping ourselves safe from that which threatened our survival. It was hard work to stay alive.

Acquiring food took great effort. With time, we improved our hunting and gathering skills, but it still took serious work. We survived as hunters and gatherers for thousands upon thousands of years until we eventually learned to farm. Farming was much more efficient than hunting and gathering but it still took immense effort. The Mesopotamians built the first basic irrigation system around 7,000 B.C., but the first large-scale irrigation system didn't come until 4,000 B.C. Before then, we had to bring the water to the crops. Tractors didn't come around until the 1880s. Before then, it was mostly all done by hand. As much as farming was a major advancement for society, it did not make the production of food easy.

We worked to survive for the first few hundred thousand years of human existence. We hunted, gathered, and farmed food. We collected water. Around 200,000 years ago, we started making clothes to protect ourselves from the elements. We made tools to make life easier. They helped us make houses that protected us from the threats of nature. We harnessed and maintained -and eventually built- fire.

It took work to live. There were consistent and difficult tasks that needed to be completed to survive.

If we wanted to live, we had to *do*. Survival took *doing*.

Doing became ingrained in our DNA.

Doing is what we learned to *do*.

Fast forward thousands of years, and in the industrial nations, we see human beings working, driving, eating, drinking, and sleeping. We run errands, pay bills, and play games. We work some more, eat some more, and drink some more.

Even for those blessed to have most of their human needs met rather simply, we still exist in a state of doing most all day, every day.

Then we do some more.

In general, the more we do, the more we have. And, in general, humans like to have more. More houses, more cars, more food. We want more vacations, more experiences, more excitement and more sex.

Our history of doing has turned us into human *doings* instead of human *beings*.

Although we've evolved a long way from our primitive selves, we still have a need to do.

There are innate human needs that will always be required for our survival: sleep, eat, drink, excrete. We need to meet these needs on a regular basis. We also need to reproduce.

We sleep for a third of our time on Earth. Although we don't fully understand why we need sleep, we know it's necessary.

Yet, many of us neglect sleep to do more. Many even consider a lack of sleep a badge of honor.

And we need to eat. We might not need to eat as much as we like to eat, but we need to eat. It provides us with energy, vitamins, minerals, and nutrients that our body requires to function.

And we need to drink water as our body consists of 70% water.

We also need to go to the bathroom. Our body must expel its waste.

And, if we want the human species to continue, we need to reproduce.

These were the foundational human needs we had when we started our physical journey at least 6 million years ago. Remarkably, we still have these same needs today.

Back then, we needed to dedicate most of our time to meeting these needs and improving our chances of surviving. Surviving was pretty much all we did early on. Sure, we probably had lots of sex, and spent some quality time around the fire and with the stars, but there was a lot we had to do early on. Over the years, we've gotten much more efficient at surviving. We've now progressed to the point where there are places in the world where our survival is almost guaranteed. Millions of people worldwide can access water with the turn of a knob. They have electricity running to their house to power appliances and tools. They have stores that carry all the food they desire.

And, at the same time, there are places in the world where people are still working to survive all day, every day. People are still carrying their water and hunting/gathering their food. The disparity between how humans live is now wider than ever.

While we can acknowledge the differences in lifestyles and living conditions around the planet -and can even do our part to support the underserved- the only thing we truly have control over is ourselves. We're going to focus there. On the self. In particular, those living in countries where they are blessed to have freedom and flexibility in regard to how they live.

Because, in many parts of today's world, we no longer need to spend all of our time working to survive. We now have time to spend on ourselves.

A few thousand years ago, it took hours to get food and water. Today it takes a few seconds. We used to spend the majority of our time working to meet these needs. Today, many of our needs are automated.

With a few dollars a day, we can immediately have all the food we require.

We can turn a knob and access clean water.

Or flip a switch and get energy.

We've even developed systems to keep us safe while we comfortably sleep at night.

Through these progressions, survival is now easier than ever before.

We no longer need to worry about staying alive. There may be moments of threat, struggle, and adversity, but in general, our survival is now guaranteed.

Survival has become a right for those in the developed world. Since we no longer need to spend our time working just to stay alive, we now have the freedom to spend time how we choose.

The odd aspect of this "progression" is that many people still choose to spend their time working. Working has become so ingrained in our DNA that we still work, even when we do not need to. It's what we do. We're doers.

We take pride in our accomplishments and all that we've done. We often define ourselves by what we've done and what we **do**.

Doing is a large part of what we look forward to and often what we reflect upon.

It's one of our favorite topics of conversation. We love talking about what we've done and what we're going to do.

What we **do** is one of the biggest aspects of who we are. What we do and what we've done, affects our perspective, emotions, abilities, and so much more. Our doings have a massive impact on the person who we are.

Doing is necessary and will always be a part of the human experience. We will always **do**.

Our doings have the ability to teach us and inspire us while placing us in a state of flow, bliss, and awe that motivates us to continue living fully. **Doing** is both necessary and beautiful. Many of the most powerful aspects of life involve **doing**.

But, there's a major difference between **doing** and *being*.

Doing will always be tied to the human experience. However, we're acknowledging that there's far more to **doing** than what you **do**. It's all about the energy you're doing *from*. Let's examine this aspect of doing.

Why do you do what you do?

Is it due to habit? Maybe it's what your parents did, and you learned to do it from them without thinking much about it.

Maybe you do what you think you're supposed to do. Or maybe, what you think you need to do.

How often do you consciously decide what you want to do? And when you're doing whatever you're doing, how present and aware do you remain while doing it? How do you do it? What energy do you do it with?

The awareness you have around your doing, and *how* you do what you do, are just as important as *what* you do. Having complete awareness of what you're doing puts you in the present moment. With this present moment, conscious awareness, your energy, focus, and attention, are all fully there in the now. Your energy is centered, focused, and grounded. You're not scattered. You're all right there. In this place, you can show up fully.

Your awareness of what you're doing also greatly affects how you do it. Do you do it with love and gratitude or resentment and negativity? Do you *get* to do it or do you **have** to do it? What energy do you do it with? Are you rushing and hurried or at peace in flow? Are you lighthearted and fun or serious and stuffy?

How we do whatever we are doing might be more important than what we are doing. You will continue to do, for as long as you're alive. What can change is how you do it.

Chapter 1 Summary

Recap:

- We have always done, and we will continue to do. It's part of being human.
- What you do plays a major role in who you are.
- What you do isn't as important as how you do it.
- How you do something is largely based on the energy and awareness you do it with.

Questions to consider:

- Why do you do the things that you do?
- What are the primary energetic/emotional states you generally do from?
- How aware are you when you're doing?
- If you were free to do whatever you wanted to do, what would you do?

Challenge:

- Track the energetic/emotional states you're doing from and how present you remain while doing it. The practice of simply tracking the state you're doing from, and the presence you're doing it with, will support you in doing from more harmonious states and doing with greater presence.
- Each night, for 1-2 weeks, record 5-10 things you did that day and the energetic state you did it with. Then, give it a presence ranking from 1-10, with 1 being no presence and ten being full presence.
- At the end of each week, look back on your records and reflect. What correlations do you see between the energetic state you did from and how present you were while doing? What else do you notice?
- How can you do from more pleasant energetic states with increased presence? (Answer for yourself, but keep reading to learn more.)

CHAPTER 2

Work

We've created a culture whose priority is work. Reprioritize and align your work.

"Your work is going to fill a large part of your life, and the only way to be truly satisfied is to do what you believe is great work. And the only way to do great work is to love what you do."

-Steve Jobs, American business magnate and co-founder of Apple Inc.

"The greatest thing money can buy is financial freedom."

-Damien Thomas, British Actor

You need money.

Our society has been established in a way that requires money. Most everything costs money. Especially housing and food.

Sure, there's alternative options of hunting and gathering food, growing a massive garden, or begging people to give you food, but you need food. If you're not gathering and harvesting your food, and you're not begging for it, you need to buy it. Food costs money. And healthy food costs even more money.

Sleeping is free, but you need a place to sleep, and most places to sleep cost money. There is always the option of being homeless and not paying for shelter, but the list of downsides is too long for me to consider this a viable option.

That said, I did live out of my Xterra for a few years and have friends living out of their vehicles now. It's a solid option as this can be a great way to save money and live on the cheap with maximum freedom and flexibility. Even then, you need money for gas and occasionally for parking. But these costs are far less than the standard cost of housing.

Nevertheless, in our current society, we do "need" money. Granted, we don't need nearly as much money as most people think we need, but we need money.

And, the primary way we make money is by working. When we provide value, we are generally compensated with money.

There are almost unlimited ways for us to make money, as we can do physical work, mental work (based primarily in our brain), or interpersonal work (based largely on connection and emotional intelligence). We can make money on investments. We can win money. Or we can do mundane, monotonous work that is not yet being performed by machines.

It doesn't really matter which technique you use, as long as you make some money. The majority of people make the majority of their money through what we call work.

The beauty of work is that there are as many different forms of work as there are ways to fill our bellies. Most everyone reading this book has the ability to choose a form of work that is aligned with the life they want to live.

This is one of the biggest steps you can take to excel as a human being, living fully alive: align your work with the life you want to live. Align your work with who you are at the core of your being. Find a job that is aligned with your essence. Or, if you can't find a job that's fully aligned, create one.

However, to align your work with your ideal lifestyle and the core essence of your being, you first need clarity regarding what kind of lifestyle you want to live and who you are at your core.

There are many aspects that go into creating your ideal lifestyle and aligning your work with your core being, but some big questions to consider include (my answer below each question):

How many hours would you ideally spend working each week?
- I enjoy most of my work and ideally spend around 30 hours working per week.

What are your gifts and natural abilities?
- Perspective, passion, creativity, coordination and agility, social skills, critical thinking.

How flexible do you want your work schedule to be?
- It's a balance for me. I thrive with scheduled time but also need flexibility. I need a medium level of flexibility.

How much work related stress are you willing to take on?
- Almost zero. I don't really do stress.

How much money do you need to make?
- $50,000 annually

How much money do you want to make?
- $250,000 annually

Where do you want to live?
- On the beach in San Diego.

How do you want to dress?
- In clothes I feel alive in. Chill, comfortable, cool, beachy vibes.

What do you like/love to do?
- Learning, growing, having new experiences, surfing, skiing, writing, yoga, cooking, meditation.

What time do you want to wake up? What time do you want to start working?

- I'm more of a night person than a morning person. 7:00am wake up. Start work at 9:00.

What makes you most excited?

- Learning and growing, teaching and supporting others, new experiences, being stoked on life, love.

What would you do if money was not a factor?

- Much of what I do now. Spend time with my kids and loved ones, teach, write, support, play, cook, eat, be.

Answering these questions will help you develop an image of the lifestyle you want to live. When this image is clear and calls you loudly, you can find, or create, a job that supports this lifestyle.

The Japanese have a concept called, "Ikigai" which translates to "your reason for being." Your Ikigai is the area where your talents, passions, societal needs, and what you can be paid for all overlap. Generally, when something is needed, it has value. You can make money by doing things that are needed. But if you have a talent for sitting on a couch and love sitting on a couch, but no one needs you to sit on a couch, you can't make money sitting on a couch.

However, if you focus on the first three aspects of the Ikigai equation -talents, passions, societal needs- and find a talent and passion that meets a need of society, there's almost always a way to monetize it. If you can't figure out how to monetize it, find someone to help.

Ideally, we can all find (or create) our Ikigai and create a lifestyle we're excited to wake up to.

Unfortunately, most people still prioritize jobs that make the most money rather than jobs that make the best quality of life.

Our priority is financial, with the assumption that once you have the money, you can create the lifestyle. What we generally fail to acknowledge is the sacrifices that are made to make the money. One of the biggest sacrifices is generally lifestyle. It's hard to make a big salary without working most of the day, almost every day. There are exceptions, but well-paying jobs are generally difficult, with high stress, high expectations, and limited flexibility.

Quality of life is often sacrificed with high paying jobs.

When we're striving for a big salary, our life can easily revolve around our job. In order to climb the corporate ladder, we often need to forfeit our independent freedom of living. We work when they tell us to work and do what they tell us to do… all in the name of promotion. What we fail to acknowledge is that signing the big contract often signs away our freedom, autonomy, and time… which are three of our most valuable possessions.

When I was running the school I co-founded and co-directed, I sacrificed my family, lifestyle, hobbies, friends, relaxation, general wellbeing, and most of my time. I was doing something that I loved many aspects of, and I was doing it for purely positive reasons, but I lost my balance. It wasn't healthy. I started losing my family. I worked 80 hours a week and was rarely able to separate from the stress of keeping a new school alive. Monday through Friday was dedicated to the school. I took half of Saturday off, then worked most of the day Sunday. I forfeited my freedom.

Shortly after leaving the school, I saw how massively important a healthy work-life relationship is.

I experienced the dichotomy between working all day, every day, and balancing work with play.

This is one of the most important balances to find in today's society: the balance between work and play. The balance between freedom and making money. The balance of autonomy and salary. The balance between living in alignment with your highest self and doing the work you need to do to make the money needed to live the life you want to live.

Where do you fall with this balance? Are you prioritizing your lifestyle and taking time to play, or are you dedicating most of your sunlit hours to work?

Let's check in on your day-to-day lifestyle.

What do you do on a daily basis?

I'm not talking about the ski trip to Vail or vacation to the Cape aspect of the lifestyle you get to enjoy a few times a year. I'm talking about the random Tuesday in February. What does your life consist of on a regular basis? How do you spend Monday through Friday? How do you spend your waking hours?

If you feel good about the work aspect of life, you're on a good path. When we find a job that provides inspiration, enjoyment, growth, proper financial compensation, and a schedule that compliments the life we want to live, we're on a path to *being*.

If you dread Monday, and are miserable by Wednesday, only to drag through Thursday, so you can coast through Friday, you may want to consider re-evaluating what you are doing with the work aspect of your life.

There are 120 total hours from Monday-Friday. You spend a third of these hours sleeping. If you work a 40 hour a week job, it consumes another third of your total Monday-Friday hours. That doesn't take into consideration the time it takes to get ready for work, commute, or debrief. When you work 40 plus hours a week, your job can easily consume the majority of your waking hours.

Which can be a good thing. I've been consumed with jobs in healthy ways and found that we can experience freedom within the structure of work. It can provide the outline for a routine that allows healthy habits to thrive.

There is a time and place for high demanding work.

But I've also experienced the opposite. I've seen work entirely monopolize my day-to-day living. In friends, I've seen work consume minds and wear down bodies while exhausting emotions and overpowering freewill.

It's a fine line between having a healthy and unhealthy work-life balance.

The work aspect of life's equation is complex. There are so many aspects to consider.

Let's look at work from a financial perspective.

We work to make money. If we didn't make money, we probably wouldn't do the work. In return, one ratio we're trying to put in our favor is the amount of money we make in relation to the amount of time we work. We want jobs that give us the most money for the least work. Unfortunately, most part-time jobs don't pay well. Minimum wage is just not livable, it's not sustainable. So, we end up going with full-time jobs. The problem is that full-time jobs take a full amount of our time.

It's beautiful when you find part-time work that pays like full-time work.

It takes time to build the skills to reach the consultant level, but consultants generally have control over how much they work and make well over $100 an hour. It's good work.

But there is an abundance of other great part-time jobs out there. One of my close friends got a job buying and selling coffee for a business that pays him $50,000 annually to do about 20 hours of work a week. He goes into the office one day a week and puts in the other time at home.

He had a vision for the lifestyle he wanted and worked to find a job that accompanied that lifestyle.

Work is a critical aspect of the journey to *being*. I've seen too many beautiful people get stuck in 40-hour a week jobs that leave them miserable the majority of the week. This bleeds over to their daily life, causing them to drink more, take longer to debrief after work, and just chill with the TV at night. There are millions of people who work all day, watch TV all night, and repeat the next day. They exist in the cycle of working and debriefing for years on end.

This work and TV lifestyle is arguably the most common lifestyle in the world today.

A percentage of these people mix in a visit to the gym or dinner at a restaurant, but in general, they've succumbed to the fact that they work 5 days to live for 2.

How can you sacrifice five-sevenths of your time? How can you sacrifice your daily happiness to be enslaved 5 days a week? How can you justify spending a third of your adult life doing something you don't want to do?

From my perspective, it feels like we should be enjoying ourselves on a continual basis. Life is too beautiful, too precious, and too short to spend our time doing things we don't like to do.

We need jobs that give us time to connect and have experiences with our family, and jobs that allow us to enjoy life on a daily basis rather than a weekend basis. We need jobs where we can utilize our talents and skills while having a positive impact on the world and ourselves.

Growing up, the two jobs that most appealed to me (outside of playing professional baseball) were journalism and teaching. I decided that teaching provided the better lifestyle, while writing could remain a great hobby and passion.

Over the course of 12 years, I taught a variety of grades and subjects, in a variety of schools, all across the United States. I almost always looked forward to work. I enjoyed my time teaching and generally left work feeling inspired.

I then took a few years to pursue the dream of opening my ideal school. With my co-founder, we built a team, developed the program, raised the money, gained approval, and made SOUL Charter School the first school approved by the San Diego County Office of Education in 15 years. While it was a dream come true to launch my ideal school, I quickly learned that running a first-year school was primarily miserable. While I enjoyed most of my work, it was all-consuming. The work/life balance I previously had was quickly lost.

My family time shrunk to a total of 30 minutes in the morning. Once or twice a week, I'd get home in time to eat dinner with my family before putting the girls to bed and getting back to work on the computer. The other 3 nights a week, I got home after the girls were already sleeping. I would try to take Saturday off before working all day Sunday.

Yet, it wasn't even the lack of time with my family that was the biggest problem, it was the stress I was under when I did have time with them. I couldn't be present. I was always thinking about the next deadline, the next do or die task, an issue with a student, or whatever else was going on that week.

Work became my identity. It was what I thought about, what I did, and how I spent my time. On the occasions when I got to spend time with friends, they asked about the school. It was what I talked about when I wasn't working.

After opening the school, I slowly started to realize how toxic it was becoming for me. I'd lost my work-life balance. In the process, I lost myself. I grew unhealthy as I became a human **doing**, running from one task to the next, lost in the world of work.

Luckily, I was able to get out. I walked away, healed myself, and started working to restore my work-life balance.

Leaving the school that I worked for years to start was one of the hardest things I've ever done. It was painful. Creating a school that could revolutionize our nation's outdated education system was one of my biggest life dreams. It was a goal I worked for almost a decade to manifest. Bringing my vision into reality, then leaving it, felt like the death of a family member in many ways.

Yet, it was one of the best moves I've ever made.

It gave me my life back. I got back to doing daily yoga and meditation. I started spending tons of time with my daughters. In the first few months of post CEO life, I grew a garden, brewed beer, went skiing, golfed, surfed, spent time with friends, took a vacation, went camping, saw a few concerts, and started to write again. I became a great father.

I got my life back.

I started to *be*.

But it was a tough transition. I had grown so engulfed in doing that it was hard to relax. For the 4 years leading up to me leaving the school, I spent all my time doing. I had become a great doer. I got work done fast so I could move onto the next task. I multi-tasked. Always. And I was good at it. I could do technical tasks and creative tasks. I solved the big problems and the day-to-day issues. I held the mission and vision and continued to steer the ship. I was important. Everyone around the school knew and appreciated me. They were grateful for the work I did. Some even looked up to me.

But I was quickly becoming someone not worth looking up to. I was losing myself. I forgot how important it was to be in balance. I lost track of the things that mattered most.

I became a human doing.

When I left the school, I went through a period of re-evaluating my self-worth and identity. Being the CEO, Co-Founder, and Director of SOUL had become my identity. It was where I found my self-worth.

Yet, I was a phenomenal human being before I ever started to work on SOUL. I was already complete and whole. I didn't need to prove anything to anybody. I didn't need to impress anybody or live up to any expectations. In many ways, I was a better person before I started the school than I was while running the school.

This is true for all of us. We don't need an important title to have self-worth. Who we are is not our job.

After leaving the school, I acknowledged how much of my self-worth I placed in my job.

The title.

The salary.

But these details change. They are not where our worth or value lie. They are not who we are.

After leaving SOUL, I had to explore my inner world and re-find myself. I had to remember who I've always been and who I always will be. I had to reconnect with myself and relearn that I already am enough. I don't need to do anything, to prove anything, to anyone. I don't need to do anything to make anyone proud.

I just need to be me.

I am enough.

And so are you.

You don't need a title to make you. You don't need a big salary, and you don't need all the stress and problems that come with it.

Leaving a "good" job is hard. It's hard to leave money on the table. But I continue to see examples of the old adage proving true, "money doesn't buy happiness." We've heard this for years. I remember hearing this as a child and almost every year since. It still holds true. I see it all around me. The majority of people I know, who are making great money doing work they don't care for, are not as happy as those working jobs that support the lifestyle they want to be living.

Now don't get me wrong, we need money. Princeton University did a study that set the tipping point at $75,000. It made the claim that there was a direct correlation between happiness and income up to $75,000. At that point, it was found that we had all the money needed to do most everything we needed and wanted to do. $75,000 brings financial flexibility -and borderline financial freedom- without the stress and struggles of higher salaried jobs.

They claim that $75,000 annually provides the best money to happiness ratio.

It makes sense.

Money is freedom. The more money we have, the more options we have. It's nice to have options. The problem is, depending on what we're doing to make money, and how many hours we're working to make money, we may not have much time left to take advantage of the additional options the money provides. Although money does give us options, the making of money often interferes with the ability to enjoy these options.

So, there's a balance. One option is to make as much money in as little time as possible. Ideally, in a way that has flexibility and autonomy.

If we work too much or too stressful of a job, we can easily lose balance with ourselves and our family. If you don't make enough money, your options as to what you eat, where you live, and what you do, become limited. In general, the less you make, the more limited your options become.

You don't want to limit your options, so you have a desire to make money. However, if you make money doing something you love, and have some degree of financial freedom, then you're doing great. You don't need more.

If you're not doing great, if you're not doing something you love or have any degree of financial freedom, then you can reflect on the work aspect of your life, re-evaluate what you're doing, and what you want to be doing. You can start making the changes necessary to move toward a place of doing something you love.

There are two other aspects of our job that are worth considering.

The first is an intrinsic desire most humans have to contribute to the greater good. We naturally want to contribute. We want to help. And, we want to be acknowledged for the good that we do and the contributions we make.

This likely comes from the centuries we spent in tribal settings, working together to survive. When we contributed, it supported our survival and improved our standing within the tribe. If we were in tight with our community, our chance of survival increased. If we were ostracized, our chance of survival diminished. After thousands of years, the desire/need to contribute became ingrained in our DNA. It became part of being human.

Fast forward a few thousand years, and the desire to contribute to the greater good is now a universal aspect of the human experience. It's part of who we are.

When we incorporate this foundational human desire/need into our work, the work feels good. It's fulfilling. We're doing our part and contributing to the advancement of society. This not only feels good personally but like it was in the tribe, it's noticed by those around you. The world experiences the benefits of our work, and we feel good about it. It's mutually beneficial.

At the same time, as we shift toward existing in a state of being fully alive with increased awareness, presence, and consciousness, it becomes increasingly difficult to do work that's not aligned with who we truly are. If your work isn't aligned with your morals, ethics, or values, it doesn't feel good. We need work that feels good. In order to be fully alive, our work needs to align with our authentic self, as well as our morals, ethics, and values... all while contributing to the greater good. When we do so, we are left with a feeling of being fulfilled professionally. This is a huge step toward being fully alive.

Professional fulfillment is a feeling that's more tied to what we're doing rather than how much we're paid for doing it. It's generally a byproduct of feeling good about the work you're doing. There's an element of being appreciated in the equation (and this appreciation is generally tied to the financial compensation we receive), but it's a small piece of the puzzle. The bigger puzzle pieces are based around what you're doing, where you're doing it, who you're doing it with, when you're doing it, and how much the doing interferes or contributes to everything else you want to be doing.

Another major element of the job aspect of life is how much you enjoy it. Do you enjoy the work that you complete each day? Are you interested in the work that you do? Do you like your employer? Do they treat you well? How about your boss and co-workers? How are the customers and clients? Does the job continue to provide opportunities for personal growth? Does it remain fresh and exciting?

These are all relevant and important questions to ask.

After asking these questions (and hopefully finding answers), you can take inspired action to make the changes you desire. Ideally, you can find, or create, a job that balances your interests and skills with a solid time/money ratio and a positive work environment.

When you work a job in alignment with these aspects of yourself, you are on your way to being fully alive.

When you work a job that consumes your time, requiring you to do things you don't want to do, with people you don't want to do them with -or is unpleasant for any other reason- it puts you on the path of living as a human doing.

If you want to thrive as a human being, you need to critically observe the job aspect of your existence. Does your job serve you? Does it contribute to the lifestyle you want to live? Does it encourage you to be the person you want to be?

If the answer to these questions is yes, then congratulations! You're on a positive work path.

If not, I recommend going back to the first set of questions in this chapter. What kind of lifestyle do you want to live? How many hours do you want to work a day? What are your skills? What are your talents? Where does society have a need? What is the best way for you to make the most money in the least amount of time? What inspires you? What motivates you? Go back and answer these questions as honestly and authentically as possible. Write down your answers. Sit with them. What can you do to make these ideal answers your waking reality?

One of my friends left his corporate job to start a business where he goes into organizations and plays games. He helps them improve their company morale. It's a new form of corporate team building he's offering. He plays games for a living and is now happier than ever.

Another friend recently quit her job and bought a camper van. She found a basic, entry-level job that allows her to work remotely and live simply and free. She's not making a ton of money, but she, too, is happier than before.

Then there's Eddie, who just shifted his focus from real estate to starting a church he is deeply passionate about. He's selling his real estate and starting to do what he loves. You see it in him. He's living fully alive.

I could continue going on with examples of people who have changed their lives by changing their job. It's one of the most concrete things we can do to start living more fully alive.

This said, changing jobs can be scary. However, we all know how detrimental it is to live out of fear. Not having enough money for rent is scary, but we don't want this fear to prevent us from moving toward our passion. At the same time, we don't want to be in a situation where we don't have the money we need to survive.

If you need a job change, you can start applying for new ones and wait to leave your current employer until the new job arrives. Start working on a passion project at night and on the weekend. That's how I started the school. I held my teaching job and built the school on the side.

Eddie's still doing some real estate while he gets the church's finances stabilized. He's just not doing as much of it.

You can cut your expenses, simplify your lifestyle, and put in some hustle.

Creating your dream job isn't easy, but it's some of the most important work you can do. Start building it on the side. Start small. Let it grow organically. Then, when it's time to switch to the passion full time, you can do so from a stable place of peace.

All of the happiest people I know enjoy their job. Those who are thriving, fully engaged, and alive, have jobs that they love. Many of these people formed a vision and created the job themselves.

Creating your dream job is an act of self-love. It's a great form of self-empowerment, growth, and development. It's a lot of work. But it's some of the best work you can do.

If you can create a clear vision for the work part of the life you want to be living, you can take inspired action to create it. But it needs to be clear. You need to feel it. Start to embody it. Feel it inside you. Then, feel it manifested in physical form. How does it feel? Use this feeling as a driving force that motivates you to create the work you dream of bringing into the world.

Bringing your passion and purpose into the world appears to be the pinnacle of the work aspect of life. This purpose can be referred to as your eco niche.

We see every aspect of the plant and animal kingdom fulfilling their eco niche. Ants have a specific job to do, and they do it perfectly. As do ladybugs, spiders, squirrels, and bears. All species of the animal kingdom fulfill their eco niche perfectly. They do exactly what they were made to do. As do all plants.

Bill Plotkin is an expert on this topic who beautifully explains the concept in an article he published on his website (www.animas. org) titled, "Soul Encounter and Eco Awakening". In this article, he explains:

> "The mysteries to which I refer here concern, in their essence, ecological place or niche — and in particular the fact that the young of all species are *born with* an understanding of their place in the world. By *place*, I do not simply mean geographical location or habitat. Rather, I mean a creature's ecological niche — its function, role, or "profession" within its community or ecosystem. The young of all species, in other words, already know at birth how to be members of their species. This innate knowledge includes basic-yet-vital items such as how to move around, what to eat and not eat, how to avoid predators, and how and when to mate and with whom. But by far the most important knowledge they are born with is *how to contribute to the world their unique skill or offering*. They, in other words, are born with what we might call ecological purpose, an implicit knowledge or apprehension of their place or niche in a wildly complex and differentiated world of multiple habitats and countless species. They are born with all the capacities and knowledge they need to at least begin to serve the world in a way no other creature can — including how they can further develop or co-evolve their own niche. They do not have to be taught or go through an initiation process to uncover this knowledge. Although birds and mammals learn a lot of behavioral specifics from their parents and primary social group, most of the capacities that enable them to function as members of their species are innate. The newborn of species *other* than birds and mammals — 95% of all species — receive minimal to no parenting beyond being conceived and birthed. They are born with all they need to know to have a good chance of survival, to be who they are, and to provide the "ecological functions" only they can."

He goes on to quote Meade before providing further explanation, "Given that such mysteries are demonstrably true for other species, how could we doubt something comparable is true for us?

In the contemporary world, we tend to believe that most everything we know we learned from others — parents, other family members, teachers, books, the internet, and so on. And indeed we have learned quite a bit this way. But we, too, like all other species, are born with certain innate knowledge of our unique place in the world, of our ecological niche, of what some older traditions called our destiny or our genius (Meade, 2016). The problem is that we are not conscious of this knowledge at birth because, after all, we are not conscious of *anything* during our first couple years. And by the time our conscious self-awareness develops — somewhere between our third and fourth birthdays — we are more than busy with other things to be conscious of, like the enchantment of the other-than-human world or how to be a member-in-good-standing of a particular family and peer group and a particular culture or ethnic or religious group. Learning these things is the natural priority throughout our childhood and early teen years. But — and here's the rub for us humans — by the time our conscious knowledge of self and world is established in our mid teens, we have strayed a long ways from our deeper, innate, unconscious knowledge of self and world, which is now obscured, buried, unremembered. It's still there within us, but we cannot consciously access it and we might not even know it exists. Consequently, as soon as our basic cultural and ecological education is complete, it comes time to "remember" the knowledge we were born with: our particular, destined place in the world, our original personal instructions for this lifetime."

There's a lot here as he's written entire books about the concept of finding your eco niche, but the basic concept is that by connecting with our true nature, we can find our specific purpose on the planet. We each have unique gifts and abilities that can benefit humanity. As you connect deeper with yourself, your gifts and abilities awaken. You begin to remember who you are and why you are here. In remembering these critical aspects of your being, you live more aligned with your true self. Living in this place will begin to reveal your purpose, your eco niche.

The best job you can have is bringing your eco niche to the planet.

The work aspect of life is complex. You're trying to balance your skills and interests with the lifestyle you want to live and a healthy money-to-work ratio… all while trying to bring your eco niche to the world.

Creating your dream job isn't going to happen overnight. There's a lot of work that needs to be done, on a lot of different levels, in order to get there. That said, you can begin working toward it today. Start to create a vision for the work you want to be doing and the life you want to be living, and start taking inspired action toward manifesting the vision in reality.

Take one step toward aligning your work with your ideal lifestyle. Then take another. They say every overnight success is 10 years in the making. Keep taking those steps. Enjoy the journey. Then, when it's time to leap, do so with peace and confidence. Stick the landing. And take off running, living fully alive, as you bring your purpose to the planet.

Chapter 2 Summary

Recap:

- In our current society, you need money to meet your needs.
- When you provide value you are generally compensated with money.
- There are endless ways to provide value. Find a way that inspires you.
- Align your work with the life you want to live.

- Strive to find your Ikigai and eco niche.
- Your work is not your identity. It's not who you are.
- We have an intrinsic desire to contribute to the greater good.

Questions to consider:

- How do you spend your time? Do you have a balance between work and play?
- How much money do you need to make annually to feel financially free?
- What are your talents and passions? How could you monetize them?
- Is your work aligned with the lifestyle you want to live? How can you make it more aligned?

Challenge:

- Find your Ikigai. List 10-20 of your passions and skills. Then list 10-20 societal needs. What appears on all three lists? Which of these items can you be paid for? How can you turn these passions and skills into a career? Create a plan to start transitioning into your Ikigai.

Next level challenge:

- Vision Fast
- Go into the woods for 2 or 3 days without food. Sit with yourself and the land. Ask to see your eco-niche.

Integrating the Past

*It's hard to be fully alive now,
until you have peace with the past.*

"Living in the moment means letting go of the past and not waiting for the future. It means living your life consciously, aware that each moment you breathe is a gift."

-Oprah Winfrey,
American talk show host/Author/ Philanthropist

"Heal the past, live the present, dream the future."

-Mary Engelbreit, American Artist

Now that we've gone through the work aspect of *being* (which provides the money you need to meet your human needs and do the things you want to do), there's one other major piece we need to address before you can fully step into your *being* and live fully alive. In order to be fully alive in the present, you need to be at peace with the past. While there are a variety of paths you can take to finding peace with your past, there's a smooth trail that leads from forgiving, to processing, to integrating.

Forgiving, processing, and integrating happen more so simultaneously than they do in sequential order. In order to forgive an event, you need to process it. And often, in order to process an event, you need to forgive and integrate it.

The separation from my wife is a strong example of how these three phases exist in unison. This process is explained more fully below but in short, as I processed everything that happened which led to our separation, I was able to find forgiveness and peace. This forgiveness and peace allowed me to integrate the learnings, lessons, and discordant energy of the separation. Integrating these aspects of it allowed me to find greater peace and forgiveness. All three phases support each other.

This process begins with mindset and perspective. You can perceive every event that occurs as happening either *to you*, or happening *for you*. When you perceive events as happening to you, you are generally in a victim mentality. When you perceive them as happening for you, you are generally in a place of abundance. The first step is shifting the mindset to accept that everything has a place. It's all for a reason. There's always a lesson or take away that can ignite growth and development. There's a change to make, a new perspective to hold, or a new path to walk.

When one job is lost, new doors open. When I left the school, it gave me the opportunity to save our town's 100-year-old hardware store while pursuing my passion for writing. These major changes had a beautiful impact on my life and would not have been possible if I had stayed with my school. Because I held a positive mindset of growth and expansion, I was able to find the beauty in the pain.

If you believe in a benevolent universe, then it all belongs. It's easy to find peace.

If you don't believe in a benevolent universe, there's still something you can take away from the experience. It might be harder to find peace if you can't find an understanding of why it occurred as it did, but peace is still an option.

For each experience you perceive as difficult or challenging, you can allow the experience to hurt you mentally and/or emotionally, knock you down, suppress you, and put you in a state of discord or pain. Or, you can learn from it, find the purpose in it, embrace it, and harness its energy as a catalyst for improvement.

This is more of a mindset than anything. It's a mindset of growth and development rather than stagnation and suffering. It's seeing things as an opportunity to do work and evolve rather than an opportunity to sit in sorrow, anger, or frustration. You can either get in the driver's seat, moving at life with an ambition to grow, improve, and optimize your earthly experience, or you can passively go along for the ride, with distraction, detachment, and discord.

With the mindset of embracing and learning from all that arrives, there is little forgiveness that needs to occur. You accept experiences as they are. They are greeted and met as they arrive, allowing you to understand, process, and integrate them quickly and smoothly. This mindset gives you peace with occurrences as they occur.

I had a great example of this occur recently when I went out for a morning surf in some big-time waves. A monster set came through and caught everyone inside, crashing hundreds of gallons of water on our heads. When I finally emerged from the pounding, I saw my board 30 feet ahead. Realizing my leash broke, I started racing for the board. I grabbed hold of it just as the next wave broke, ripping the board from my hands again, before holding me down even longer than the first wave. I swallowed water and struggled to catch my breath. I started swimming for the channel as two more waves rolled me. I don't know how many more I could have taken. I had no breath left, my muscles were fried, there was no board to float me, and I was a few hundred yards from shore. After a short panic, I collected myself, got to the channel, and floated on my back while catching my breath. I slowly made my way back to shore with little left in the tank. It was the first time I'd really been scared out in the water.

When I finally found my board, it was thrashed.

I saw Timmer -a friend who I was surfing with- a few moments later.

I said, "Woooo! Dude! That was gnarly. What an experience. I panicked for a second but got myself together and made it out. It was good for me. It was scary as hell, but it was good, man. And I got my board back! I think it's repairable."

I used the experience as an opportunity for growth and improvement rather than allowing it to get the best of me. I'll now err on the side of staying farther out on big wave days, secure my leash more firmly, and know that I just need to make it to the channel, so I can breathe.

I could have been beaten and scarred by the experience. I could have been angry that the board was wrecked, that Timmer brought me out on such a big day, or anything else I could have chosen to be mad about. I could have allowed the experience to negatively affect me. Or, I could use it as a learning experience and grow from it, allowing the experience to have a positive effect instead.

It all starts with mindset and perspective. Are you a victim of the occurrence or did the occurrence happen for you? Did it happen *to* you or did it happen *for* you? This aspect of the equation is fully dependent upon your perspective.

When you accept the philosophy that everything belongs, you can search to find the purpose in everything that occurs. You can process, find peace, and integrate in the present rather than hold onto occurrences and carry the effects far into the future.

The integration piece referenced above is a major step in clearing the past. If you process and find peace but don't integrate the lesson, or the energy of the event, it will remain within you as discordant energy. This discordant energy will continue to rise up and cause difficulty in your life. Integrate the significance of the event by sitting with it. Feel the energy. Feel the sadness, the heaviness, the silver lining, and all other aspects of it. Go through it. Allow the energy to flow through you. Go into it. Embrace it.

Ask yourself, what does the energy feel like?

Why is it there?

What does it need?

How can it be embraced?

Can you use it for inspiration?

How can this energy help you to grow, develop, or expand?

As the energy of the event is integrated, it becomes part of you. It adds onto your being. It gives you new wisdom and perspective. In this place, your higher self can embrace the beauty of the occurrence and honor it for the growth and development it provided. Acknowledge that it helped you grow and evolve. Bow your head in thanks and gratitude.

This process can be completed with each experience that throws you off center or triggers something within you.

When you create the habit of integrating major events as they occur, you're freed to be more present and alive in the moment.

However, in order to get to this place of processing your reality as it unfolds, you usually need to clear some pieces in the past.

For me, this began with working on events that were more recent. I acknowledged there were stories I held toward people or occurrences that led to negative emotions toward these people and events. I started by finding peace there.

What was my part in it? What were the lessons I learned or could learn from this experience? How could I grow from it? What did it show me? Why did I feel negatively about it? Do I need to feel that way? Does that feeling serve me? Is there another perspective I could hold? Can I see how this served me? Can I get to a place of holding gratitude for this occurrence?

In answering these questions, you can process events from a reflective state that supports progression and peace. From this place you can create new understandings of people and events from your past. You can find appreciation and gratitude for them that allows you to move forward, free of resentment, animosity, frustration, or any other negative emotion.

And, you learn and grow from the experience.

Getting to this place may take some work, but it's some of the most important work there is to do.

After working through all the current pieces of discordant energy you feel within, you can start working back through older events you still hold discordant energy around. This can take some digging. Grab your mental shovel and get ready to do some work.

Every experience you endure carries a corresponding energy. You often carry pieces of this energy with you as you move forward. When you don't understand, integrate, or find peace with an experience, you carry discordant energy of confusion, frustration, or anger.

As you integrate, or heal, the experience, this energy is aligned and released.

When doing this work, there are steps of integration you can apply to support your process.

By understanding these steps, you can identify where you're at on the journey to integration, and do what you need to complete that phase and progress to the next. In my years of work with integrating experiences within myself, studying the topic, and supporting family, friends, and students to do the same, I've found the 8 phases of Integration to be as follows:

8 Phases of Integration

1. Acknowledgement And Acceptance Of Discordant Energy

In this phase of integration, you need to see, feel, own, and accept that there is unintegrated energy within you. You can reach this acknowledgment by gaining awareness of your triggers, negative thoughts, negative actions, or any other behavior that is not in alignment with your highest self. These triggers, upset emotions, negative thoughts, or any behavior that is not love and light, are generally trail heads that can lead you to find any unintegrated energy within you. This unintegrated energy is generally tied to events and experiences of your past.

Finding this discordant energy can sometimes take digging. Other times, it's right there, messing up your life, obvious for all to see. But more often than not, our body does an effective job of suppressing this energy and hiding it away. These hiding pieces are often referred to as the shadow. Carl Jung considered all aspects of the self that are unconscious, the shadow. The shadow exists outside of the conscious mind. Hence, the digging.

Fortunately, we live in a world with an abundance of techniques for helping you uncover the unconscious. Each of the techniques have different benefits and will have different effects on different people. Some of the more popular (and effective) techniques for uncovering the unintegrated energy within you include:

- Therapy
- Meditation
- Group work and Intensive weekends
- Plant-based medicine journey
- Vision fast/time alone in nature

2. Desire To Integrate Unintegrated Energy

With the awareness that you have unintegrated energy within you, you can see what you do that is not in alignment with your highest self. Often, the difficulties you experience in your life today are products of unintegrated events from your past. Unintegrated energy will continue to flare up and cause discord until you integrate it. Eventually, you gain awareness around these energetic flares and become aware of when you hurt someone, when you speak untruthfully, or produce any other action that causes pain to someone else. You gain awareness around the discord you experience in your life and want nothing more than to live in a blissful state of peace and harmony.

With the awareness that you have caused pain to others and that you have unnecessary discord in your life, you can not only acknowledge and accept that you have work to do, but you can develop a deep desire to do the work. You can get to the point where you never want to ever hurt anyone again, and you don't want to experience any more unnecessary discord.

Moving this discordant energy through you takes work. It's tough. Without the desire, you're probably not going to do it. Finding this desire can lead you to do the work, integrate your negative energy, and live aligned with your highest self.

3. Acknowledgment Of Strengths- Self-Love

It's hard to dive into the pains and struggles inside you if you don't have a strong platform to jump from. This platform, our foundation, is established by acknowledging and appreciating all the beauties of yourself. Acknowledge the work you've done. Thank the struggles you've overcome. Honor the strengths and abilities that are part of your being.

Establishing a strong connection with the strengths, abilities, and essential essence of your being provides a foundation of self-love that enables you to vulnerably explore the depths of your past. It gives you the confidence to revisit events you don't want to revisit and supports you in sitting with yourself to release them.

Everyone has aspects of their being to love.

What are your gifts and strengths?

What makes you different from others? How are you unique?

How do you act and behave in a way that you like?

Find the love for yourself.

4. Observation And Understanding Of Pains

In sitting with events of your past, you will often experience the feeling of discordant energy. It doesn't feel good. It feels unsettled. Unresolved. It's confused or frustrated. In order to integrate this event and align its energy, you need to first observe the discordant energy. Why is it discordant? What is it frustrated or upset about? Where does the confusion lie? What negative beliefs are you still carrying around this event?

As Michael Brown repeatedly states in, *The Presence Process,* "the only way out is through." He explains that the only way to get out of the pains we experience is to go through them. Feel it. See it, understand it, find peace with it, and release it. Why is this feeling within you? Where does it come from? What caused it? Why do you still hold it? The more you can see and understand the discordant energy within you, the more effectively you can move through it and release it. This cannot be done by avoiding the event. You need to go into it and move through it.

If I use the separation from my wife as an example again, we can see that if I had avoided the event, and refused to go into the heaviness of it, the discordant energy from it would remain within me. By allowing myself to go into this energy and work with it, I was able to move through it.

5. Forgiveness For Wrongs Done And Pains Caused

Through the process of going into, and working through, the pains of your past, you will face aspects of the pain that are on you. There are wrongs you've done, poor decisions you've made, and pains you've caused.

In acknowledging and owning the pieces that are yours, you can learn from the experiences, improve upon your flaws, and grow. You can use the flaws of your past as catalysts for growth.

However, in order to do so, you need to forgive yourself for each of the "wrongs" you've done. You can't integrate the energy and grow from the experience when you are still holding onto negative thoughts or emotions around it. The experience needs to be forgiven. At the highest level, this means forgiving not only yourself but all other parties involved.

You don't need to personally call and forgive everyone you've held negative thoughts or beliefs toward, but you do need to find forgiveness for them. This forgiveness comes from within you. It becomes much easier to forgive others when you can own your part of the discord, learn from it, and forgive yourself. From here, you can see what parts are yours and what parts are theirs. The pieces that are theirs involve their own personal work that they have to do. This is not your work. Let their work go and find yours. Pick that mental shovel back up and keep on working.

6. Re-Writing The Mental Story

After you've forgiven yourself and everyone involved, you can re-write the mental story from a positive perspective. When you acknowledge the learning and growth that the event provided, you can find appreciation for it. Reframing the event in the positive can help with this process. It allows you to create positive thoughts and feelings around the event rather than negative ones.

Ideally, you get to the point of re-writing your mental story for every "negative" event you've experienced.

Instead of believing, "she broke up with me", tell yourself, "She freed me from a relationship that didn't serve me." It doesn't change the event in the physical realm, but it does change the energetic charge you hold around the event. As you rewrite your negative stories into positive ones, you align and integrate the energy of your past.

7. Embodiment Of New Perspective

From here, you can begin to embody the new perspective. However, simply reframing the story does not transform it in your body. There are often years of energetic ties to the old story that need to be broken. It takes work to embody the new story.

One powerful technique for owning the new story is turning it into a positive mantra that you repeat to manifest it in your reality.

As I went deep into my self-work, I found an old story where I was a victim and someone owed me something. In working through each of the steps above, I eventually got to this step of embodying the new perspective. I understood the new perspective mentally but struggled to embody it. The old belief was deeply ingrained. As I sat fireside completing my full moon ceremony, I was inspired to rewrite the old story into a new, positive mantra. After sitting with the new belief that I was working to embody, words started coming to it. Eventually, I got to the place of re-writing the old limited belief that "I'm a victim and someone owes me something," as, "I am blessed and live in abundance." This is a far more powerful belief to hold. The new mantra was repeated daily for a few months following the perspective shift. I still find myself saying it years later.

Not only did I continually repeat the mantra, but I also took concrete steps to embody it. During my night time routine, I started listing ways I was blessed throughout that day. This helped me become increasingly aware of the abundance I exist in. Through this awareness, I was able to step further into abundance, allowing myself to exist within its flow. Through these practices, I began to embody the belief of being blessed and living in abundance.

The steps taken to embody the new story will vary from story to story. It doesn't so much matter what steps you take to embody your story, as long as concrete steps are taken.

8. Living Empowered And Fully Alive

As stories from your past are re-programmed to become positive stories that serve you, you will begin to live more fully alive. There are multiple aspects to living fully alive that will be covered throughout the upcoming pages as it's a big one. As long as you hold negative thoughts or emotions toward events of the past, you cannot live fully alive in the present. You need to let go of everything that is holding you back and meet yourself here, now, with peace for the past and peace for the future. In this place, you can be fully present and alive in the moment. This is a beautiful place to be.

To further explain these steps to integration, I'll again use the example of my separation. The first two steps (1. Acknowledging and accepting you have unintegrated energy & 2. Desire to integrate unintegrated energy) were easy. I was feeling horrible, fully aware that I had unintegrated and discordant energy that needed to be processed. I was uncomfortable, ungrounded, confused, hurt, sad, and so much more. And, when I feel these ways, I'm always motivated to move through it.

My first struggle came in the third step (Acknowledgement of strengths- self-love) as my self-love had hit a low in the months leading up to our separation. It took me some time to build my self-love back up, but through camping, skiing, surfing, writing, connecting with family and friends, playing music and dancing, gardening, cooking and eating, and meditating and yoga, I built it back up. These are the things I love. They ground me and help me feel alive. They bring me to life. They remind me who I am and why I love myself.

From here, I was able to go into all the pain I had around our separation. This is the fourth step, Observation and understanding of pain. I had a lot of pain. It took a long time to sit through it all. There were many days spent alone with myself at the beach or in the woods. Sitting. Feeling. Going into everything I was feeling. I'd dig for the roots beneath each emotion. Why did I feel this way? Sometimes, when I'd get stuck, I'd use a modality to help. Plant-based medicines (especially psilocybin) were particularly effective at helping me work through the pain.

Eventually, I was able to get to a place where I could forgive myself for all the wrongs I did and pain I caused to my wife. Just as much of our separation was on me as it was her. It was hard to own all of my stuff. And, after owning it, it was just as hard to forgive myself. But I knew that I was doing the best I could with the situation I was in. I never once had ill intentions or tried to hurt her. I did my best to show up with love and light. I knew these pieces to be true, allowing me to finally forgive myself for all that I did.

From here, I was able to re-write my mental story in the positive. This is the 6th step. This was an incredibly challenging step as I had so many mental stories and beliefs around the way my life was going to be that had to shift. I had to create new perspectives and intentions for so many aspects of my life. I took days of sitting with a vision for the future before I was able to create new intentions that inspired me. With this new vision of where I was going, I could more clearly see why the past occurred as it did. I could greater see the learnings and growth that took place and the benefits that came out of it.

As the mental story was re-written, I transitioned into the 7th step of embodying the new perspective. I created and repeated mantras to help embed the learnings. As part of my night time ritual, I'd meditate on the higher perspective and welcome it in. I set positive intentions and took inspired action to embody my intentions.

In this place, I had peace with the past and felt motivated and inspired in the present. I was excited about the future. I felt like myself again (an upgraded, more evolved version), fully stoked on life. This piece of me was back to being fully alive.

Working through these steps is not easy. Getting to the place of integrating your past, to live fully alive in the present, takes great effort. Entire books have been written about most of the steps listed above as they are complex and involved. Yet, there are common threads amongst each of these steps that can be accessed through one particular modality.

The biggest thread amongst the steps to integration is the silent stillness of sitting with yourself. This silent stillness supports both reflection of your past and awareness of the emotions you're experiencing now. The more you sit in silence with yourself, the more perspective and wisdom you can gain from your past, and the more clarity and understanding you can develop around what you're feeling in the present. Sitting in silence with the self provides presence, awareness, and understanding. It connects you with your higher self in a way that provides peace with the past and perspective in the present. In this place, you can remember who you've been, who you are, and who you always will be.

If there's one skill humanity could learn to help us connect more deeply with ourselves, our planet, and each other, it's meditation. Sitting in silence is one of the best things you can do for yourself. It allows you to take control of your mind and, eventually, your reality. Meditation can create improvement in every aspect of your life. It can make you more present and aware, focus your energy, inspire peace and tranquility, reduce stress and anxiety, create control over your thoughts, and connect you with your true self.

If you want to clear your past to live fully alive in the present, the path of meditation is an extremely effective route to travel.

One of the beauties of meditation is that there's no right or wrong way to meditate. Meditation is a personal practice. There are a variety of meditation techniques out there that you can be drawn upon or you can simply sit in silence with yourself. You can listen to a guided meditation or you can do a walking meditation. You can focus on your breath or on connecting with the higher. Again, there's no right or wrong way to meditate. The key is finding what works for you.

For, when you do surrender to the silent stillness of meditation, the submerged emotions of your past are given the space to surface. Here, you can greet them. Say hello. Develop a relationship. Understand each other. Reach an agreement. Find peace. And let them go.

In this silent space, you can also find a knowingness that is hard to experience within the noise of life. Things start to make sense. You can see more clearly. You can hear what you say and feel what you feel. Perspective can appear, and wisdom can develop. You can find a knowingness as to why things occurred as they did, why you said what you said, why you feel what you feel, and why you are where you are. This wisdom is inside you. You simply need to get silent and still enough for it to emerge. In this silence, you begin to know. You know what is and will be. You know what's not and never will be. You know what you are and always will be.

However, getting to this space of stillness takes practice as your mind has lots of thoughts it loves to think. Learning to quiet it (and possibly even control it) is not only one of the most difficult tasks there is to master but arguably one of the most important. As long as your mind continues to run, you cannot experience the silent stillness of peace. Stillness is found within the silence of the mind. In this stillness, we find peace, knowingness, connection, and understanding. This is a glorious place to find.

Meditation is the path to find it.

Your past holds all that you've done, thought, said, and experienced. It holds every relationship you've had, success you've celebrated, and struggle you've endured. It holds your learning and growth, your family and friends, your sets and settings, and your loves and losses. This has all combined to create the person who you are today. The better you understand your past, and the more you integrate it, the more fully alive you can live today.

Chapter 3 Summary

Recap:

- In order to be fully alive in the present, you need to be at peace with the past.
- Peace can be found through forgiving, processing, and integrating.
- Develop a positive perspective.
- Experiences carry corresponding energy.
- Walk through the steps of integration to align the energy of your past.
- Meditation is a powerful tool for aligning your energy and finding peace with your past.

Questions to consider:

- Do you perceive events as happening for you or happening to you?
- What events in your past have you yet to find peace with and integrate?

- Which of the steps in the integration process is most difficult for you? Which is easiest?
- What's your relationship with meditation? How could it be improved?

Challenge:

- Select an event from your past that you do not have peace with -that you have not integrated the energy of- and work through the steps of integration to integrate it. Upon completing this process, reflect upon it. How did it feel while doing the work? How does it feel now? How do you feel now in relation to how you felt before doing the work? Are you now inspired to integrate another event?

Next Level Challenge:

- Find (and integrate) unintegrated experiences in your shadow. These are often events from your childhood that you've hidden away or rationalized. Internal Family Systems therapy is an effective approach for finding these pieces of your shadow. Plant based ceremonies are another. Sign up for a ceremony or do some Internal Family Systems therapy.

Being

Progress from a human doing to a human being.

"It doesn't matter what you choose, what matters is the energy with which you choose it."

-Caroline Myss,
American author of 5 New York Times Best Sellers

"Nothing is more precious than being in the present moment, fully alive, fully aware."

-Thich Nhat Hanh, Vietnamese Buddhist monk/Peace Activist/founder of Plum Village Tradition

"It takes courage to grow up and turn out to be who you really are."

-E.E. Cummings,
American Poet/Painter/Essayist/Author/Playwright

You are in a constant state of being. You can consciously choose to stop doing, but as long as you remain alive in earthly form, you will always continue to be.

You may or may not remain conscious of your being, but even when you are unconsciously living, you are still being.

Being is an inescapable aspect of the human condition.

What varies is the energetic state from which you are being.

How do you feel when you have a list of tasks to complete and not enough time to complete them? You know time is limited, but you feel a need to get it all done. So, you run around, frantically trying to check items off your list. As you race from one task to the next, your body temperature rises, your thoughts scramble, and your emotions become agitated. You make mistakes and find yourself forgetting things as you go. You're overwhelmed. You work harder instead of smarter. Things spill or break. You become frustrated, and the list is still not finished.

Now think about a Sunday morning when you have nothing but time. You take a walk while sipping on your tea and taking in the nature around you. You enjoy conversation with a loved one, freely, with no agenda, before consciously deciding what to do next.

Can you feel the energetic difference between these two states of being? In the first example, you are frantically doing. You are in a high-energy place of low pleasantness. In the second example, while you are still doing, it comes from a balanced energetic space of pleasantness.

In the first example, we see doing. In the second example, we see being.

Life is lived- and experienced- through the energetic state in which you are being. While your energetic state generally has some variance from day to day, and even within each day, you are still a creature of habit. The energetic states in which you spend the most time become the most comfortable and easily accessible, which leads you to spend even more time in these states. The more time you spend in positive states, the more time you will continue to spend in positive states. The same can be said for negative states.

As Newton's first law of physics explains, an object in motion remains in motion unless acted upon by an outside force. When you set yourself in motion in a positive state, you can remain in a positive state until you're acted upon by an outside force. In the case of your energetic state, the outside force is generally life. Something happens. Depending on how we react or respond, it could force us into a different energetic state.

According to the Mood Meter from the Yale Center for Emotional Intelligence, our energetic states range from low energy and low pleasantness to high energy and high pleasantness. By tracking where you land on the Mood Meter, you can begin to see patterns emerge as to the energetic state of your being.

If you don't want to take a few weeks to track yourself on the Mood Meter, you can sit with the Mood Meter (you can pull up the image online), read the energetic states it outlines, and feel your response with each of them. Which states most resonate with you? Which don't? Which states do you want to experience more of? Which states do you want to experience less of?

Take some time to think about the feelings, and the energy, associated with each of these different energetic states. How does it feel to be excited? What about curious? Disappointed? Playful?

We often begin our day in one energetic state then transition to other states throughout the day as it's common for us to react to the environment around us. We may find ourselves in one state with one person and a different state with another person. Our state of being may make a major shift when one thing occurs, then another shift when something else occurs.

As you progress on your journey back home, you gain skills that support you in remaining more consistent with your energetic state.

We'll cover many of these skills throughout the upcoming pages. For now, I'd like to examine the energetic states from which you enter your being.

Let's begin by reflecting on the following questions:

Who do you choose to be when you wake up in the morning?

Who do you choose to be in the face of adversity?

Who are you with kids and the elderly?

Who are you with the rich and the poor?

Who do you choose to be when you pass a fellow human being, dying at the intersection, with a sign in his hand asking for help? (That's a tough one. For all of us. I'm not saying there is a right or wrong way to respond, but it does give us an opportunity to explore how we respond.)

There are so many aspects to the energetic state from which you be.

How do you treat others, and how do you treat yourself?

Who are you when you wake up, and who are you when you go to bed?

Who are you with family, and who are you with friends?

Who are you when met with disagreement or the word no?

Who are you with success or accomplishment? What about struggle or failure?

Who are you when things are good, and who are you when things are hard?

Your answers to these questions reveal the person you are. This is who you have chosen to be.

Begin looking out for opportunities to consciously respond to your environment rather than unconsciously react. How do you want to respond? Who do you want to be in this moment?

As you gain awareness around your reactions, they evolve from being reactions to responses. When you reach the state of consciously responding to each aspect of your environment -rather than passively reacting to it- you gain control over your energetic state of being. This is a powerful place to be.

Existing in this state of being in control of your emotional state of being begins with a choice to embrace your emotional body. You must accept that being alive means you are going to feel. It's a foundational aspect of the human experience. However, as you learn to see and understand your emotions of low energy and low pleasantness, you can hold these emotions in a way that allows them to exist without dominating your energetic state. They are a part of you, but they are not who you are. They have a place, but it's not front and center.

Front and center lies your highest self. Your true essence.

The more you connect with this core aspect of your being, the less space you hold for the weaker aspects of self you've acquired along the way. As you experience the beauty of remaining aligned with your highest self, you lose the desire to exist in any other state.

You still allow your emotional body to feel what it feels, but you see and acknowledge the feelings without allowing them to alter your high vibrational state of alignment.

Rather than existing in a state of subconsciously reacting to the occurrences around you, you choose to consciously respond to the world around you. This change is based on awareness. By remaining aware of the world around you and the emotions within you, you can choose how you respond and what energetic state you remain in. Awareness allows you to respond as an observer of the environment rather than as a victim of the environment. Rather than feeling that something happened to you, you can simply acknowledge that something happened. You can then respond neutrally, without judgment, and ask yourself if this is something that needs to affect you? Does your energetic state need to be affected because this occurred?

The occurrence may even trigger feelings inside you. From this state of awareness, you can observe those feelings and ask why you were triggered. Why did this occurrence make you feel this way? What do you need in order to move past these feelings?

My car was recently hit while parked. They smashed in the front drivers side wheel well, leaving noticeable damage. I could have chosen to get upset, hunt down the culprits, and force them to fix my vehicle. Or, I could acknowledge that it's just a vehicle. It's a thing, and things get hurt. They break. I made a simple shift to my mindset and acknowledged that being upset about my vehicle did nothing to serve me. It did quite the opposite. It made me frustrated and heavy. When I became aware of these feelings, I was able to shift them.

This space of awareness is incredibly powerful. It puts you in a relationship with the emotional state from which you meet the world. Rather than having your emotions control you, you can control them.

You can choose to acknowledge your emotions, work with them, relate to them, understand why they are there, harness their energy, transmute it into positives, and grow your power. Or, you can ignore your emotions, deny and suppress them, and allow their energy to flare up to create negativity or problems.

One of the biggest steps we can take in our evolution to higher states of being is increasing awareness. Developing a relationship with your emotional being, becoming increasingly present, hearing the sounds that surround you, smelling the smells that smile to your nose, tasting all the flavors from your favorite foods, feeling all the feelings your body feels.

This place of pure and absolute awareness of the self, the environment, the seen and unseen, is one of the highest states of *being*. It's a place within each of us, aligned with our true authentic selves. It's a place where we see what's in front of us, hear what's around us, and feel what's touching us. It's a place of knowingness. It's a place of balance and alignment with your highest self. A place of pure love and light.

It's a place of being fully alive.

When we're fully *being*, we're present with the current moment, at peace with the past, alive in the beauty that exists within us and around us.

When *being*, we settle into the forefront of the moment, to the space where reality is created.

Here, we're fully present in the current moment while consciously creating the next moment. We become the developer of our game and the creator of our reality. It's the most powerful place there is to be.

The place of *being* is often marked by feelings of bliss, connectivity, joy, fulfillment, and awe. You feel alive and complete as time can dissipate to create an expanse of self and interconnectedness to source.

You are, and it is.

Most of us have been here at one time or another. We've lost ourselves in physical activity or artistic creation. It's one of the reasons we love sports. It's impossible to hit a baseball without being fully present. When we dance (like no one is watching), we are fully present. We are *being*. The same goes for creating art, playing music, surfing, skiing, and most forms of sex. Sometimes cooking or eating can put us there. Reading or writing. Running. Sitting in nature. These activities can put us in a space where nothing came before, and nothing comes after. The only moment we are aware of is that moment occurring right now. We become entwined with the moment. There is nothing else. No thought, no worries, no fears, or agendas.

You are fully alive in those moments. Purely present. Being fully alive.

Now imagine taking that sensation of being 100 percent present and applying it to all aspects of your life. Think about the way you feel at the climax of your favorite song, by your favorite musician, at your favorite venue, in the most epic version of the song ever played. Take that feeling, and imagine feeling it always.

Imagine walking down the street with that feeling. Imagine having that feeling while you work or talk with a friend. What if you felt that way while eating and playing? Imagine feeling fully alive always.

That's what we're working toward here.

Take a few slow, deep, conscious breaths. Settle into your body.

Before we move into the how, there's one more lens of being we need to examine. This is being in the body.

Our fast-paced lifestyle, screens, and continual distractions take us out of our bodies. Work, life, and society encourage us to be in our head. Shows, drugs (alcohol, caffeine, etc.), processed foods, and medications all numb us from our bodies.

We exist in an environment that enables and supports us in detaching from our bodies.

Part of our work is getting ourselves back in our bodies. Connecting with ourselves. Listening to the voice within and feeling everything there is to be felt. We can evolve from accepting our body to loving and honoring our body. Evolve to feel more than you think and listen more than you speak.

When you are in your body, you grow connected with it in a way where you know what it wants, needs, likes, and dislikes. You learn to work with it in a way that is both harmonious and mutually beneficial.

Once you get in your body, you can listen to it and feel it. But it's hard to fully listen or feel when you're in your head.

An easy way to get in your body is by grounding with conscious breathing. To ground, you can simply step outside, take off your shoes, stand firmly on Mother Earth, and take some deep, conscious breaths, drawing your focus and attention into your body. Move out of your head and bring your energy and awareness inward. Release your thoughts. Feel the movement of your sternum, lungs, and stomach. Hear the sounds around you. Feel the Earth on your feet and the breeze on your skin. Take a moment to enjoy this place of *being* fully in your body.

From here, you can focus your attention on listening to and feeling the body. Where do you feel uncomfortable physically, emotionally, and mentally? Where do you feel strong physically, emotionally, and mentally?

The longer you sit in this place, and the further within you allow yourself to go, the more your feelings and emotions can emerge. Some of them are way down deep. They take some work to find. But the more you sit in your body, the closer you come to finding everything within it. Eventually, it is all revealed.

As you work through everything you've held within, you become more capable of fully feeling and experiencing the present moment. The more you release the past and fully free yourself from your emotional connections to it, the more present you become.

It's a self-perpetuating cycle as the increased presence inspires you to remain in your body to continue experiencing the presence and awareness it brings. The more time you spend being in your body, the easier it is to be in your body. As you get more comfortable in this state, you begin to spend more and more time there. You slow down a little bit. You get a little quieter. You listen -and hear- a little more. You feel a little deeper. You live a little more fully.

Being in your body is purely beneficial. It heightens your awareness, stabilizes your emotions, and places you in the present. From this place, you still think and use your brain; you're just not enslaved by it. You're aware of it rather than consumed by it. You can use it as a tool to serve you rather than a master who controls you.

As you continue to shift your attention from your head to your body, it becomes easier and easier to consciously embody your physical being. Once in there, it becomes increasingly easy to listen to and hear everything it says. What does it need? What does it want? What is it telling you? What do you need to change? What do you need to do more of? Your body knows these things.

It knows when it needs to eat, and it knows what's best for it. Slow down, connect, and listen.

It knows what kind of work it wants to do and what kind of people it likes to be around. Slow down, connect, and listen.

It knows where you're thriving and where you're struggling. It knows what's best for you and what's not. It knows which road to take, which passion to pursue, and which friendship to foster. You just need to connect with it and listen.

As you do so, you continue to grow in not only your awareness and presence but your ability to live fully alive. Being connected with your body helps you to feel all your feelings, experience with all your senses, and live with permanent bliss.

We've already covered using meditation to get into your body, but there are other access points as well. Each of these paths to *being* in your body are significant in their own way. They each serve a different purpose and give us access to our *being* on different timelines in different ways.

The use of meditation to enter the body is a slower, more gradual path. It's one that requires focus and concentration. It's a path into the body that can be accessed anywhere, at any time. While it takes time to get deep with this path, it can take you deep. You can get as far into your body in a deep meditation as you can with any of the other paths listed below. This path can be accessed by anyone, wherever, whenever. It's one of the most universal paths into the body.

Another path to being in your body is through physical use of the body. Dig in the soil. Build and create. Do yoga (which also integrates the breathing...although you can technically integrate conscious breathing into any of these techniques). Dance. Surf. Ski. Kiss. Be sexual. These are all ways to bring ourselves into our bodies. These can each ground us and bring increased awareness and presence.

Few things bring us as much awareness and presence as sex. Sex brings us into our bodies in a way of its own. The biggest difference between sex and the other techniques here is that sex involves two people. The other techniques can be done alone. Granted, we can bring ourselves into our body alone sexually, through touching and playing with ourselves, but it can be very different from the presence and awareness that we experience through making love to another.

This said, sex is not a complete, full-body awareness or presence like the one we experience through conscious breathing. Sex brings us into our physical body as intensely as anything, and sex can bring us into our emotional body, but it doesn't really bring us into our mental bodies. It brings us fully into our physical bodies, and can support us in experiencing an emotional exchange with our partner, but it doesn't necessarily bring us closer to ourselves. If anything, sex can be a distraction from feelings that are alive within us. For these reasons, while sex is a way to access the physical body, it might not be the most effective path to connecting with yourself.

If we examine some of the other physical paths to being in our body, we see that many of them may be more effective than sex. Take physical activities like surfing and skiing. These physical activities generally create full presence and awareness. If you are not fully in your body while surfing or skiing, the odds of a gnarly wipeout increase dramatically. If you are thinking about what happened yesterday or what's going to happen tomorrow while working your way down a double diamond or an overhead beast of a wave, you're in danger. These activities require complete attention and presence.

At the same time, they provide a deep connection to the environment around you. When skiing, you become one with the mountain. While surfing, you become one with the water. You are fully alive within yourself while feeling a deep connection and awareness of the environment around you.

Again, these physical activities do little to connect us with our emotional or mental bodies. This said, physical activity can be an extremely effective modality of moving emotional or mental energy through us. If energy is stuck, these types of activities can help move it.

Dancing is similar. The beauty of dancing is that, like conscious breathing, it can be accessed by anyone, anywhere. Dance is universally accessible. It also connects us to our body and can move unwanted energy.

Dance therapy, surf therapy, and ski therapy are effective for a reason. They bring us into our bodies and get energy moving through us.

The difference between the physical forms of accessing the body and the conscious breathing of meditation is in the presence vs. awareness ratio. Meditation can bring us deeply into the body while providing high amounts of presence and awareness. Physical activities can bring us deeper into the body, while providing extremely high amounts of presence but not as much awareness. The awareness in these activities is very focused on the task at hand. You're ultra-aware of that one thing, but have little awareness around what's going on inside your mind or body.

The important part of all these paths to *being* in your body is taking the experience of feeling fully alive with heightened presence and awareness and integrating it into your daily life. Recall the emotional state regularly after the experience. Feel it. Sit it in. Next time you have the experience, do the same. The more you experience this state and practice integrating it into your daily life, the more it becomes a part of your *being*.

So, how do you take that experience of being fully alive in particular moments and transfer it to all other aspects of life so you can experience its bliss permanently?

How do you live fully alive *always*?

This is a question we'll continue to tackle throughout the upcoming pages. To begin, let's go deeper into the awareness aspect of *being*.

Pay attention for the next time you're fully present, alive in the moment, aware of your *being*. Maybe it's right now reading this book. Maybe it's the next meal you eat or the next song you sing. Look for that next moment of being fully alive in the moment, where your awareness and presence are heightened and partnered with a heavy side of feeling blissfully stoked.

Acknowledge what prompted this fully alive state of *being* into existence.

What came before the beingness, and what brought the beingness to an end? What did you feel while *being*?

After experiencing and acknowledging the state of being -and hopefully taking some time to enjoy it- you will eventually return back to your head. You'll return back to an unconscious, habitual based routine.

From here, your work is twofold. The first piece is doing what we discussed above and integrating the energy and feeling of the experience into your life in the proceeding hours and days. Take the uplifting energy of awareness, presence, and bliss with you. Embody them.

The second piece is then re-gaining awareness around the next moment when you are fully alive and present in your being. Again, allow the moment of *being* to remain as long as possible. Upon completing the moment, ask yourself the same questions.

What brought on this experience of fully *being*? What caused the beingness to end? How did you feel while *being*? Then, integrate.

As you continue to move through your days, continue looking for moments of pure *being*. In doing so, the space between these moments will continue to shrink. You will slowly move out of your head and into your *being*. You'll begin to be more and do less. By simply placing awareness on your state of being, you will begin to evolve from a human **doing** to a human *being*.

There's a lot more to the equation than simply gaining awareness, but awareness is a great place to start.

Become aware of when you move into a place of doing. Notice when you're rushing, fully in your head, with your heart racing and presence and awareness lacking. We all fall into this place on occasion. The key is catching yourself when you fall. How did you let yourself get in that place? What were the factors that contributed to the frantic state? How can you prevent them from occurring again? How can you catch yourself sooner if/when it happens again?

Start placing awareness on your state of being. What energetic state of being are you in when you wake up in the morning? What state of being are you in while working? What about when you're running errands or at night before you go to bed?

What causes your state of being to shift? What causes it to improve? What uplifts and inspires you? What makes you most aware and present? What gives you the greatest feeling of stoked type bliss?

At the same time, observe what throws you off. What causes you to feel anxiety or stress? When are your awareness and presence reduced? When is your bliss missed?

Remain aware of how you respond (or react) to your environment and that which enters your field. How do you allow the occurrences around you to affect your being? Be aware of how you respond to difficult situations, beautiful situations, and all other situations. Develop awareness around when you feel best and when you feel worst.

As you develop awareness around your state of being, you start taking control of it. You learn to see the occurrences for what they are, acknowledge and honor them, and release them without taking on their energy. That is, unless it's energy that you choose to take on. If it's that blissfully stoked energy, you might want to bring some along for the ride.

In this place, you can consciously choose to remain in your preferred state of being.

Awareness of your state of being is the trailhead that leads you from living as a human **doing**, to thriving as a human *being*.

Once you find this trailhead, you can access all the lessons and learnings that exist along the way. Enjoy the journey. Take your time. Look around. There's beauty to behold. Take it in. Sit with it. Integrate and apply it.

It's a journey that will provide as many upgrades as you can handle. Open yourself to receive and prepare to do work.

No great journey is easy. It is, however, exactly as you make it.

Chapter 4 Summary

Recap:

- You are always being. What varies is the energetic state in which you're being.
- Shift from reacting to responding.
- Increase awareness to be more present and alive in each moment.
- Practice getting centered and grounded in your body. Move out of your mind and into your body.
- Use your body. Move. Play. Enjoy.

Questions to consider:

- What energetic state are you most often being in? What other energetic states do you find yourself in?
- When do you find yourself most present, aware, and fully alive in the moment? When do you struggle to find awareness and presence?
- Where do the stories of your mind interfere with the wisdom of your body? How do you know which is which?

Challenge:

- Perform an evening ceremony dedicated to being in your body. You can include the 7 directions where you turn to acknowledge, thank, and show gratitude for the north, west, south, east, up to the skies, down to the earth, and into the self. Feel the energy flow from the earth through you, into the skies, and out in each direction. Move your body. Dance. Shake. Move. Do some yoga. Sit in silence and go within. Feel your body. Activate its energy. Let it come alive.

CHAPTER 5

Being in Time

Allow your time to serve you.

"My favorite things in life don't cost any money. It's really clear that the most precious resource we all have is time."

-Steve Jobs, American business magnate and co-founder of Apple Inc.

"They always say time changes things, but you actually have to change them yourself."

-Andy Warhol, American artist

Time provides a foundational reference point for comprehending our day-to-day existence. It's the third dimension of our reality. Based on our agreed upon units of measuring time, every human being gets 24 hours per day. How you choose to spend these hours becomes one of the biggest factors in who you are.

Let's examine the primary ways we spend these 24 hours each day.

Approximately one-third of your daily time goes to sleep. There's not much you can do about your need for sleep. There are alternative sleep patterns you can grow into (which potentially allow you to thrive on less sleep), but they are not for everyone. No matter how we break it down, you need to sleep for 6-8 hours a day.

You then need to eat, drink, and go to the bathroom. These are basic human needs.

Let's start with drinking. We don't generally set time aside for drinking as we generally have a drink with our morning routine, then sip water throughout the day and maybe have a beverage at lunch or dinner. Sometimes we'll get together with friends and enjoy a few drinks as we socialize.

Drinking has become an easy need to meet as it no longer takes time or effort to get clean water in much of the world. In return, we're not going to set aside any time for drinking as it's become a pleasant part of our daily routine that partners well with other aspects of life.

As for food, we do take time to prepare food and eat.

Some of us eat breakfast on the run but let's say that we spend 30 minutes making and eating breakfast, 40 minutes preparing and eating lunch, and 50 minutes cooking and eating dinner. These are estimates that put us at two hours of cooking and eating per day.

8 hours of sleep, plus 2 hours of food, equals 10 hours a day.

For thousands of years, humanity spent most of its time working to meet its basic human needs. Most of our time went to collecting water and food, creating shelter to remain safe, and sleeping. Meeting our basic human needs used to consume all of our time. It now takes less than half of our time!

This means that you now have upward of 14 hours a day to spend as you please.

So, what do you choose to do with this time?

Take a moment to sit with yourself and answer this question. How do you spend the rest of your time?

There are so many ways you can answer that question.

Personally, I'd say that I spend my time learning and growing, connecting with and supporting others, shining my light, playing with my hobbies and passions, and having a lot of fun. These are my priorities, so they're how I spend my time.

I learn and grow by reading and writing, parenting, teaching, talking with friends, reflecting, meditating, and experiencing. I connect with, love, and support others through parenting, sitting with my men's group, spending time with family and friends, and remaining open to and aware of opportunities to connect with new people. I shine my light by writing, creating, helping others, teaching, and living fully alive. I have fun by cooking and eating, surfing, skiing, hiking, dancing, playing with my daughters, and playing music.

This is how I choose to spend my time. The specific doings that fall under each category will vary from day to day, but I spend most of my time, on most of my days, pursuing my intentions of learning and growing, connecting with others, shining my light, and having fun.

So, how do you choose to spend your time?

With the standard job taking 8 hours a day, most people are left with about 6 hours of "free time" a day.

But 6 hours of free time a day isn't bad. Most of us would love to have 6 hours of free time each day.

The problem is that most people who work traditional 40 hour a week jobs spend an hour a day commuting to and from work (although remote work is finally changing this for millions of people). They then take 30 minutes getting ready for work and 30 minutes debriefing from work. This cuts their 6 hours of free time down to 4 or less.

If you add in a chore, cleaning the house, an addiction to television, playing with kids, or any form of hobby or recreational activity, and you quickly have no time left. Monday through Friday can easily be filled with work.

This is a lifestyle in which we work 5 days to live for 2.

That's a tough ratio. It's a schedule that lacks balance. It doesn't provide us with much time to nurture ourselves, pursue our passions, or sit with the stars. It's a schedule based on **doing** that lacks space for *being*.

Yet, most humans hardly notice the flaws in their schedule as we've been conditioned to believe that working is what we are supposed to do with our time. Most people spend the majority of their non-sleep time working. It's normalized and rationalized but rarely re-worked to become harmonized.

Fortunately, there are an unlimited number of alternative options as to how you can spend your time.

Granted, in order for you to gather, prepare, and eat your food in under a few hours a day, you need to make money. But there are an abundance of ways to make money.

One way to make money is with a 40 hour a week job, but there are so many alternative work options in today's world. It's becoming harder to justify spending most of your free time grinding away at work.

Leave the monotonous work to machines and find human work you love.

When you start to re-imagine the work aspect of life, you can become empowered by the possibility of creating a lifestyle that inspires you.

Let's examine a few of the inspiring lifestyles I've had the privilege of seeing along my journey.

One friend goes skiing every morning he wants. He then works from early afternoon through the evening, tuning skis. In the summer months, he's a landscaper who goes on a hike before or after work each day.

Another friend goes from country to country working random jobs. He was a tour guide in the Amazon Rainforest, worked the coffee fields in Columbia, tended a farm in northern Canada, and helped prepare for the World Cup in Africa.

Then there's Tyson, who moved to Laos, where he started a for-profit coffee roaster to fund his Nonprofit organization that brings clean water and hygiene education to the children of Laos.

Neil teaches classes at Tulane for half the year then lives in India for the other half of the year running a Nonprofit that helps improve their quality of living.

11 of my close friends got jobs at online charter schools where they work from home for around 4 hours a day. This provides them with a basic teacher salary while giving them the flexibility needed to create a lifestyle they love.

Kelly left her corporate job to start a homestead.

Eddie left real estate to start a church.

Mike left his job working with stem cells to become a fine woodworker. He hangs out with his kids when they're around, then works in his garage, building tables and chairs when they're at school and in bed.

I could keep going with examples of people who have created alternative approaches to their work. None of them work traditional 40 hour a week jobs, but each of them are thriving.

They have created lifestyles that allow them to be themselves.

They are *being* rather than **doing**.

They exist in a place of aligned balance with their true authentic selves. They enjoy their day-to-day living. They are learning and growing in alignment with their higher self, and many are serving their eco niche.

Another friend has been living out of a Westfalia for the past few years. He'll pick up odd jobs here and there to give himself a few bucks for gas and food, but outside of that, he's just *being*. He chills on the beach, surfs, reads, and writes. He sits, does yoga, enjoys conversations, and watches the sun set. He's existing purely in a state of *being*.

Now, for those with families, it's not overly easy to live out of a Westy as a perpetual beach bum. But it IS an option.

The point here is that you have options.

Although we are all pushed down the path of becoming enslaved to the machine, working 5 days to live for 2, we do have other options.

You can teach dance lessons, find a job abroad with a nonprofit organization you're aligned with, or walk dogs.

While few of these jobs pay as much as the typical 40 hour a week job, they all provide an opportunity to create the lifestyle you want to live. As your job becomes more flexible, you increase your ability to live. The fewer hours you work each week, the more time you have to enjoy yourself and *be*.

As you become more aligned with your authentic self and align your lifestyle with this authentic self, the work aspect of life becomes something you do to maintain your lifestyle, as opposed to the work becoming your lifestyle.

Or better yet, you monetize your lifestyle in a way that allows you to make the money needed to maintain the lifestyle you want to live.

When your work supports your lifestyle, you generally have the opportunity to *be*.

You can be a beach bum. You can be a parent. You can be an artist, a skier, a traveler, a photographer, musician, dancer, or anything else you want to be.

When I was a kid, I was always told that I could be whatever I wanted when I grew up. I always thought this meant I could have whatever job I wanted to have.

I wanted to be a baseball player.

I worked hard and developed a great swing. My team was in the state championship when a scout told me that if I was 4 inches taller -or right-handed- I'd be the top draft pick in NY. I was 5 foot 10, which would put me at second base in the upper levels. But I was left-handed which meant I couldn't play second base in the big leagues. I played some ball in college, but that was as far as I made it.

I thought my parents had lied to me. I worked as hard as I could, and I wasn't able to be a baseball player. At least not at the professional level. I now acknowledge that not making it pro doesn't mean I can't be a baseball player. If I still wanted to be a baseball player, I could hold that intention and pursue that dream. There are men's leagues that play a few times a week.

Garrett is a beer rep who plays baseball a few times a week. He manages both "The Dudes", a competitive men's baseball team that plays every Saturday, and the "Ding Dongs", a co-ed softball team that won the championship a few years in a row. He's 40 something years old and still plays ball at least 3 times a week. It's what he loves to do. It's who he is. So, he created a lifestyle that allows him to be a ball player.

My parents were right. I can be whatever I want to be.

You can be whatever you want to be.

The key is creating a vision for what you want to be. Then, holding that intention while taking inspired action to create your vision in reality. Create a step-by-step plan that will allow you to live the life of your dreams. Take inspired action to follow your plan. Manifest your vision in reality. Join Facebook groups and other online forums related to your dream. Connect with others in that space. Learn everything you can about it. Develop the skills that you need. Embody and live it.

The point here is that you don't need to spend your 14 hours of free time a day working. It might be the safe path -it could even be perceived as the easy path- but it definitely doesn't have as much upside as other paths and is generally not as enjoyable.

So, how do you create a new path more aligned with your authentic *being*?

It starts with asking what kind of life you want to live. Who do you want to be? What do you love? How do you want to spend your time? What would you do if money wasn't a factor?

Sit with these questions. Find answers that deeply resonate. Feel the excitement of pursuing that life.

Then, accept the reality that creating a new path is easier said than done. Weigh the pros and cons of pursuing a new path or staying the traditional path. Creating something new requires a leap of faith. It's scary. It's a lot of work. It's hard.

And, it's exhilarating. It's freeing and exciting, and deeply impactful. It will teach you and force you to grow. It's fun.

But many people have bills and expenses that lead them to believe they can't leave their job. Others feel they are making good money and can't fathom taking a pay cut to change careers. Another percentage of the population has worked hard to learn their job and now have it "pretty easy." The learning curve has been summited, and they are on cruise control. Doing something more exciting, or finding a job that provides a better work-life balance, feels scary. They'd have to "start all over."

In these cases, where your mind is set and you're realistically not going to change your job, the question then becomes, how can you *be* while working your job? How can you *be* within the day-to-day grind of making ends meet? How can you *be* while running errands or sitting in traffic?

The goal isn't finding 15 minutes of meditative time a day to center and ground yourself. The objective is not to *be* while you're taking a yoga class or dancing at a concert. Those are freebies. Those aspects of being are built into your existence to show what's possible. They are crutches that help you find that state of being so you can incorporate it always, in all ways.

You can take the feeling you experience in these states and carry it with you into other aspects of life. If you want to take the yoga bliss vibe with you into the kitchen, that's easy. It's a bit harder to bring the yoga bliss vibe into the corporate cubicle.

If you're spending your time doing things that don't align with the energetic state you want to be in, you need to change the things you're doing.

Generally, your hobbies and activities are easily aligned with your highest state of being.

Many jobs are not.

If you're spending your time working a job that makes it hard to be the person you want to be, you probably need to find a different job.

As Steve Jobs said, "My favorite things in life don't cost any money. It's really clear that the most precious resource we all have is time."

It's ironic that we're sacrificing most of our time for money. It feels like sacrificing our time for money should be an old, outdated mindset that we've evolved past. And, in some ways, it is. We're evolving out of it. More people continue awakening to the reality that in this lifetime, you get one life to live. Many of these people are taking inspired action to live fully. And at the same time, billions of people are still fully in the paradigm of trading their time for money.

However, if you are one of the billions still trading your time for money, know that you do not need to remain within this paradigm.

Yes, creating a new lifestyle that aligns your time with your passions and purpose can be frightening and arduous.

But there are not many greater ways to spend your time than doing what you love.

There are a few other aspects of time usage I'd like to touch on.

The first of these is having fun.

I know many people who take little to no time to have fun. While this is most likely a byproduct of our work focused society, there are no excuses for not having fun. Having fun is a foundational aspect of being human. Part of our purpose is to enjoy ourselves and all the beauty life has to offer.

It doesn't matter what your fun is. As long as it gives you that full-body pleasure of bliss and presence. Being in this state raises your vibration and makes you feel good. You can then take this heightened vibrational state with you into whatever else you are doing. The more you put yourself in this high energetic state, the easier it is to maintain it. By dedicating time to having fun, the rest of your time benefits. Ideally, you can then incorporate that state of fun into everything you do. There is fun to be found in all of it when we take the time to look.

There are songs playing that we can dance along to. There's humor in the child that we can laugh along to. There's rain to dance in and puddles to jump in. There's food to play with and nature to laugh with.

There is a lighthearted playfulness existing around us that we can tap into when we slow down and exercise our muscle of play.

Another relevant aspect of time usage is self-care. Again, this is often overlooked. Like everything, what self-care looks like for you is different from what it looks like for me. For me, my ideal form of self-care may be skiing; for you, it might be a massage.

Self-care is taking time to love yourself, to be with yourself, and take care of yourself.

While the forms of self-care that are most effective for you will range from person to person, there are certain techniques that are universally beneficial.

I take 30-60 minutes before bed for yoga and meditation. This happens every night.

I then take 30 minutes most mornings for yoga and meditation as well.

Yoga and meditation are probably my favorite/most effective forms of self-care as they work on my physical, mental, emotional, and spiritual bodies.

I journal a few times a week for my mental and emotional bodies, I surf for my physical and spiritual body, I talk with friends and therapists for my emotional body. I do acupuncture, energy work, sound healing, hot/cold plunges, and breathwork. I sit in sacred ceremonies, spend time alone in nature, and perform my moon work. Each of these forms of self-care work on different parts of my *being*. Depending on what your *being* wants/needs, you can implement different forms of self-care.

It doesn't so much matter what forms of self-care you implement as long as you are taking some time to care for yourself and work on yourself.

It's also worth noting that not all self-care is sexy. Sometimes, it's sitting with your emotions and having a deep, full-bodied cry. Other times, it's going through intense counseling or therapy sessions. Self-care can come in all shapes and sizes. Sometimes, it's light and fun, other times, it's heavy and difficult. The heavy and difficult forms of self-care might not be as much fun as the lighter forms, but they're just as significant.

Again, by taking time to be proactive with your self-care, your other time will benefit. By taking the time you need to move energy through you, ground yourself, process the events that occur, and keep your mental, physical, emotional, and spiritual bodies in a high vibrational place, you can be fully present in your body and live more fully alive.

The final aspect of time we'll address is the concept that time is not linear. A year for a 5-year-old is not the same as a year for a 50-year-old. An hour spent in a stimulating conversation is not the same as an hour watching paint dry or an hour of intense physical activity. When we skydive, time is warped. When making love, time can almost stop. Psychedelics change time in ways of their own. They can bring you to a time before time and a time of all time, where all that ever was and all that ever will be, is all right now.

Time expands and contracts from moment to moment based on a variety of factors, including but not limited to engagement, presence, stimulation, difficulty, and the release of adrenaline or other chemicals. Some moments expand for what feels like lifetimes, while other moments pass before you catch them.

To make the most of your time in the physical realm, you need to be present to the moments in life. There are beautiful moments occurring daily that you can emerge yourself in with full presence and awareness. Time slows down in these moments. You feel the beauty. You lighten and glow. When you slow down enough to fully experience the life occurring around you, your time is multiplied. It seems counterintuitive: slow down and move slower to experience more. The counterintuitiveness shows how limited our concept of time is.

As you move faster to accomplish and do more, you experience less. The faster you move, the more you miss.

This is why time moves so slowly for kids. They are fully present, taking absolutely everything in. Always. They're not upset about something that happened yesterday or worrying about something coming up tomorrow. They hardly even comprehend the concept of yesterday and tomorrow until around five years old. Kids exist in the eternal moment of now. Fully present and aware. Always. In return, their time moves slow.

As you slow down to embrace the beauty in your moments, your senses are stimulated, your gratitude and awe multiply, and your enjoyment magnifies. You become more fully alive.

It's about turning your time into true moments. Not just the Saturday-night-at-the-concert-with-friends moments, but the rocking-out-to-your-favorite-song-on-your-harmonica-while-sitting-in-traffic type moments. It's noticing the majestic tree off the trail and sitting with it. Hearing the elderly couple talking about what they want to do this weekend while standing in line behind you and giving them a pleasant recommendation. It's showing up and participating in the moments occurring around you, acknowledging that they are happening for you.

When you can show up in this way and turn your time into true moments, life slows down, and you live more fully alive.

Between the lands of yesterday and tomorrow, exists the perfection of now. This is a moment that is generally pleasant. There is beauty around you and within you. One of your jobs is to slow yourselves to speed that allows you to feel it. See it. Embody it.

There is a place between days where time stops. Here we are completely present with connected alignment to all which we are. It's a place where stress and fear have been replaced with peace and love. It's a place where we see the perfection as it unfolds in alignment with all. This is a place that you can strive to exist in each day.

Just a few minutes in this place can feel like an hour, as time in the present is generally non-existent.

The beauty is that you can visit this land from wherever you are. With practice you can transport to this space while sitting in traffic or standing in a checkout line. You can exist here while walking down the street or playing with your kids. The more you go here, the easier the trip becomes. The bridge shortens with each journey. And, like most beautiful places, it becomes addictive. You fall more in love with each passing visit. You eventually desire to live there. Permanently. And, with practice and dedication, you can do so.

Upon setting up residency in the eternal moment of now, you make major strides to existing in a space of *being*.

Chapter 5 Summary

Review:

- Based on basic human needs, you need to sleep and eat. Outside of that, you get about 14 hours a day to spend as you please.
- Create a vision for the life you want to live. Take inspired action to manifest it in reality.
- Bring the stoke of being fully alive with you from the blissful states to the mundane.
- Having fun is the most fun way to spend your time.
- Practicing self-care is one of the most powerful ways to spend your time.
- Time is not linear. Increase presence to slow it down.

Questions to consider:

- How can you modify your schedule to support you in living the lifestyle most aligned with your highest self?
- What would you do with your time if money wasn't a factor?
- How much time do you spend practicing self-care? How do you love yourself?
- What is your relationship with time? Do you see it as abundant or limited?

Challenge:

- Spend a day consciously trying to slow down time. Enjoy the activities that make you most present and aware. Feel the time warp. Stretch it out. Allow the moments to last. Observe the details. Later that night, reflect on how you spent your time. When did time move the slowest? When did it move fastest? What can you do to slow it down even more? How did it feel to slow down time? How much did you live in that one day? How can you create more days where you maximize the amount of time you spend living?

Play

Ignite your childlike essence, have fun, and be alive.

"We are never more fully alive, more completely ourselves, or more deeply engrossed in anything, than when we are at play."

-Charles Schaefer, American psychologist

"Play is the highest kind of research."

-Albert Einstein, German-born theoretical physicist

There are some questions we may never find definitive answers to. Some of the big ones include, "why are we here?" and "what is our purpose?"

No matter where your beliefs on these questions lie, it's hard to exclude some form of "enjoyment" in your answer.

If we do not reincarnate and only live one single life (which is hard for me to wrap my head around as Newton proved that energy cannot be created or destroyed, only transferred from one form to another), then it's easy to claim enjoyment as our primary purpose.

If we only get 85 years in human form, we should do all we can to maximize our time and make the most of it. Enjoy yourself. Experience. Play. Eat and drink. Laugh and love. Have fun. Enjoy.

But, if we do reincarnate, if we do come back to life form multiple times, possibly hundreds, or thousands of times, it's easier to make an argument for our purpose being some form of cosmic journey.

Maybe it's a journey to experience all aspects of life or to connect back with complete alignment with Source, or maybe to create a Heaven on Earth.

But what could heaven on Earth be, if not enjoyable? If connecting back with Source isn't blissful enjoyment of love, then what is it?

Every way I look at it, I see enjoyment as one of our primary purposes on this planet. It feels like enjoyment is one of our goals in physical form.

It's much harder to make an argument that our purpose is to make money.

There are many possible answers in regard to our purpose that are easy to discard.

Is our purpose to sleep? Nope. Sleep is a necessity. It can be enjoyable. But it's not our reason for existing.

Is our purpose to eat? No. Although food is one of the great pleasures of earthly form, it's definitely not the reason we're here.

Is our purpose to survive and reproduce so we can maximize human potential? Possibly. Though this answer lacks depth and sustenance, sexual intimacy is one of the greatest forms of enjoyment we have.

Is our purpose to learn and grow, to align our energy, connect back with Source, and transcend human form? Possibly, but again, what is growth if not enjoyable?

From my perspective, enjoyment is undeniably part of our purpose.

How can you possibly live a balanced life without enjoyment as part of your balanced equation?

For me, enjoyment is a foundational aspect of why we are here.

We need to enjoy ourselves. Enjoyment is part of being human. So, let's talk about enjoyment. Play.

What do you do for fun? This is not a hypothetical question. Rather, it's a question that we all need to answer. How do you find enjoyment? How do you play? What do you do for fun?

Let's begin by grabbing a piece of paper and writing device and creating a list of 20 things in life you sincerely enjoy. I recommend doing this right now before you go any further. Grab a pen and paper and create a list of at least 20 things you sincerely enjoy.

Fortunately, there are endless ways to enjoy yourself in human form. This list is simply a starting point. That said, this is your starting point. The activities and experiences that you enjoy are different from others. The clearer you get on your activities, the easier it is to bring them into your daily life.

I had a long conversation with one of my spiritual teachers about the intense lifestyle I prefer to live. I like to eat and drink, ski the steepest terrain, surf waves, use plant medicines, travel the world, have sex, do yoga, meditate, talk, read, write, have raw and vulnerable conversations, try new things, get some sleep, and repeat. I read a lot about the monks and holy men who abstain from consuming life's pleasures. I started to question whether I should be removing some of these enjoyments from my life. Should I try to simplify and live more "monk like"?

I asked my teacher about this concept expecting to hear that I need to stop enjoying herb and sex if I want to continue progressing on my journey.

Her explanation resonated deeply and has stayed with me since. What she said is that there are many different paths. The path of the monk is slow and gradual. They do not face many struggles nor overcome many obstacles. Rather, they remove all temptations to live a life of devotion and worship. This is a slow, gradual path that may or may not get you where you want to go. There will be few setbacks. You will most likely remain steady. The growth will be slow.

Instead of encouraging me to pursue this path, she encouraged me to continue eating, drinking, playing, and experiencing as intensely as I desired. And while doing so, she reminded me to remain conscious of everything I do, everything I consume, and everything I experience. Learn from all of it. Gain awareness around every aspect of my daily existence. View each experience as an opportunity for growth. Develop a healthy relationship with all of it. Remain in control of all urges and desires. Become a master of my domain.

This path will have ups and downs, and, like the slow and gradual option, it may or may not get you where you want to go. But it has the potential for being a much steeper learning curve. There's a greater upside. Granted, this path can bring more "pain" and "struggle", but it brings more enjoyment as well.

This is the path for me. I like enjoyment. I enjoy play.

I've learned that I like to play most every day.

The play looks different from day-to-day, but there is generally some form of play included in each and every day I'm alive. Today I started my day by playing with yoga and meditation before playing in my garden. I'm now sitting on my pergola, overlooking the ocean, playing with words. From here, I may eat my first food of the day. To make food can be to play with it... especially when using a playful perspective. The same can be said for eating. I will most likely jump in the water later today and play in the waves. I will play Duck Duck Goose or hide-and-go-seek with my daughters. I'll hopefully get to play in bed tonight.

Fortunately, play can be found in most aspects of life as a large aspect of play is the mindset and perspective with which we approach the situation. Do you choose to have a playful demeanor or one of seriousness? I've been working to reestablish the balance between light hearted humor and philosophical depth as I became more serious through my work with starting and running SOUL.

As I rekindle my childlike playfulness, I acknowledge how pleasant a playful perspective can make the day-to-day doings of physical form. Living with a childlike pleasantness and playfulness helps to move us from a place of **doing** to a place of *being*. For, when we enjoy what we're doing from a place of pleasant playfulness, we exist in a fully present place of *being*.

I've yet to meet a child who doesn't like to play. Every single child I've ever met has a playfulness to them. It's part of our authentic being. However, as we grow and age, this demeanor can be easily forgotten. For some, even lost under years of pain, heaviness, and suffering. Life is so hard for so many people. For many, the childlike essence has been hidden away, in a deep corner of the psyche, protected by self-defense mechanisms that attempt to protect it. Working through all these levels of self-defense can take an immense amount of work. However, as the self-defense mechanisms are identified and addressed, the inner child is carefully set free.

Whether or not we choose to do this work and activate this aspect of our being is a choice for us to make. Either way, the childlike essence remains within us. It might take some work to uncover, but once you remember and re-engage this aspect of yourself, you can dance along with the music or play make-believe. We have the pleasant playfulness of a child within us.

The question is, how far have you been removed from this natural way of being? For some, the playfulness is still front and center, as it was when they were 5 years old. For others, it's buried beneath years of pain, hidden away, to be forgotten forever.

Fortunately, our childlike essence is never gone, just buried. By working through the traumas, stories, and struggles that have buried your inner child, you start to uncover it. The more of these distractors you work through, the more your inner child is empowered to shine.

Part of our work lies in reconnecting with our child-like, playful self.

It's seeing the world with a sense of awe and wonder. Living with lightheartedness and a skip in your step, being quick to laugh, and ready to joke.

Then there's the question that I posed earlier in this chapter: What do you do for fun?

Through my years of playing, I've found a variety of forms of play which I find purely enjoyable. Some of my favorite forms of play include skiing, playing music, golf, surfing, gardening, dancing, cooking, eating, and hanging with family and friends.

When I ski, I'm 100% present. I'm working my physical body, creating endorphins, and activating adrenaline, all while connecting to the land and nature. It's my perfect form of play.

Surfing touches on many of these same pleasure points though I'm not nearly as good at surfing, so it's not quite as enjoyable for me.

Golf activates more of the mind and less of the body than skiing and surfing, but it still includes that element of connecting me to nature. It also brings in a social element that can be lacking in skiing and surfing.

Gardening gets my hands in the earth, connecting with the soil and our food. It's grounding, meditative, and enjoyable.

When playing music, you're fully present, consumed by it. You can't really play music and be somewhere else. You can play music that expresses your feelings in a present moment rhythm and flow. Playing music can be so incredibly fun.

Dancing is another beautiful form of play. It's freedom and self-expression and connection to something outside of yourself in a way that is purely healthy. Dancing is playful and fun. And dancing can happen any time. Dance when the music's playing and dance when it's off.

Hanging out with family and friends often does little for me physically, but it fully stimulates my mind, creates laughter, and often provokes thought and the opportunity for reflection and growth. I find hanging with loved ones to be one of my favorite forms of enjoyment.

These are my go-to forms of play. My goal is to enjoy at least one of these every day as each of these forms of play refresh my soul. They help me remain fully alive. They allow me to be.

It doesn't matter what forms of play you incorporate into your daily life. It can be dancing and art or building and creating. Cook. Sing. These are all forms of play. You can play the guitar or piano. We even include the word "play" in the explanation of these musical hobbies! We "play" the guitar. The same can be said for "playing" baseball or soccer. Or "playing" with kids. Again, there are endless forms of play. It doesn't matter what form of play you enjoy as long as you enjoy some form of play.

The key is the word "enjoy". If the play becomes work, then it's no longer play. Some people sincerely enjoy working out. For them, working out could be play. But, for many, working out is work.

Work is not play.

One of my good friends is an incredible musician. He created a few albums and plays smaller shows on a regular basis. I had a great conversation with him about turning his music into a career. He explained that if he was playing music to make money, it would turn his music from play to work. We decided that he didn't want to work music; he wanted to play music.

This resonated as there is a big difference between doing something for work and doing something for play. Still, I challenged him by asking about the old adage, "when you do what you love, you never work another day in your life." He replied by explaining that if he played music for money, then he would need to do something else for play. He likes music as his play and doesn't want a new play. Again, this deeply resonated. We need play.

UCLA researchers said, "Throughout the lifespan, play supports neurological growth and development while building complex, skilled, flexible, responsive and socially adept brains."

Play is good for us. It's healthy. It supports neurological growth and helps us develop the kinds of brains we want to have.

The benefits of play don't stop here as the National Institute for Play states, "play generates optimism, seeks out novelty, makes perseverance fun and leads to mastery. Additionally, it gives the immune system a bounce, fosters empathy, and promotes a sense of belonging and community."

If this still isn't enough evidence as to why we should prioritize play, we can look at Allan Watt's perspective on the matter. He explains, "It doesn't have some destination it ought to arrive at. It's best understood by an analogy with music. Because music as an art form is essentially playful. One doesn't make the end of the composition the point of the composition. Same with dancing. You don't aim at one particular spot in the room where you ought to arrive. The whole point of the dancing is the dance… we thought of life by analogy with a journey, with a pilgrimage, which had a serious purpose at the end and the thing was to get to that end-success or whatever it is, maybe heaven after you're dead. But we missed the point the whole way along. It was a musical thing, and we were supposed to sing or dance while the music was being played."

He uses the analogy of music to share the perspective that the point of life is to play along with our environment. Take what's given to you, embrace it, feel it, move along with it, have fun with it, and enjoy it. Play with it. Dance along.

Each of these three perspectives demonstrates different reasons why play is an essential aspect of our being. It's healthy. It improves multiple aspects of our life. And most importantly, it's one of the foundational reasons why we're here.

The only downfall to play is the belief that you can't get everything done that you need to if you take time to play. You create excuses why you can't play rather than making time to play. By shifting your perspective to acknowledge that everything will be completed in divine timing, you can move at a pleasant pace, enjoying each move you make.

Play is more about how we're doing than what we're doing. It's a mindset, and attitude.

You could play a board game with your family in an ultra-competitive place, getting frustrated with your teammates for not doing well before making negative comments about the game or their performance. You get absorbed in winning as you forget that the purpose of the game is not to win but rather to have fun. In this example, you're playing to win at the expense of fun.

While competition itself can be fun, when the sole objective is winning, enjoyment is often sacrificed. While the benefits of games run deep, at their roots remains enjoyment and fun. But, like everything, even games are only as fun as you make them.

In the same way as you can take a game and make it stressful and frustrating, you can be at work, with a big deadline looming, working at a pleasant pace, whistling along, laughing with co-workers, while eating a tasty snack and bobbing to some beats. Even with the deadline looming, you can still enter work with a pleasant perspective of playfulness.

When I was younger, I worked construction with my uncle in Upstate NY. There was snow on the ground and ice all around. He'd throw snowballs, play little pranks, and was always rocking out to some classic rock. While he was making the most of the situation, I was busy complaining about how cold I was. That winter was the end of my construction career. I let it get the best of me. I allowed the environment to dictate my perspective rather than using my perspective to dictate the environment. Uncle Mike made the environment what he wanted it to be. I was too young and immature to appreciate the beauty in it.

I was coming from a place of work rather than play.

I was working with one of my favorite uncles and two of my best friends, learning lifelong skills outside in nature… and I failed to see the beauty in it.

I saw all the work and little of the play.

This goes for everything you do. It's your mindset. It's the energy you do it with.

Do you *have* to cook dinner, or do you *get* to cook dinner? Do you cook it as quickly and efficiently as possible, or do you cook it with love, fun, and playfulness?

Do you hustle to complete tasks and errands, running from point A to B, getting in and out quickly, or do you move at a pleasant pace, smiling at the beauty along the way, interacting and playing with the environment as you dance to the music of life?

Do you hop scotch through the squares drawn on the sidewalk, or do you walk right past them without really noticing? Will you roll down the hill with the kids and play tag, whistle to the birds, and splash in the puddles? Or do you feel too mature for those childish things? Maybe your clothes are too nice, or your body is too sore to play like a child.

Whatever your excuse is, it's exactly that, an excuse. Your essence wants to play. Your highest self wants to play. You just need to adjust your mindset and allow yourself to play.

As CS Lewis said, "When I was ten, I read fairy tales in secret and would have been ashamed if I had been found doing so. Now that I am fifty, I read them openly. When I became a man, I put away childish things, including a fear of being childish and a desire to be very grown up."

Play is natural to living. Ant's play, monkey's play, and people play. We are meant to play. We want to do things that put us fully in the moment, in a place that supports us in being aware and alive.

Play can temporarily disconnect us from our cloud of thoughts and allow us to fully enjoy the present.

When we incorporate a mindset of play, a mindset that encourages enjoyment of moments rather than the pursuit of destinations, we learn to enjoy the journey rather than simply desire the end result.

Play is void of time or objectives, and strong in laughter and presence. It's lacking opinions and judgment while remaining abundant in joy and wonder. Through the mindset of play, we can approach our day-to-day tasks with a childlike, playful persona, finding fun in the mundane and beauty in the basic.

Play is a practice that can become a habit. By consciously practicing the art of having fun, we learn to enjoy ourselves more deeply and live more fully alive.

The more we incorporate play into our daily lives, the more we activate our child's heart. This is a heart that likes to remain present. It easily forgives the past and has little fear for the future. It's a heart that sees the best in everyone and the awe in everything. It's innocent and pure. Loving and kind. Funny and fun. Playful. Curious. Engaged. Alive.

As you age, it becomes increasingly important to redevelop a relationship with this playful side of yourself. Life can be difficult. But playing tag is not difficult. It's fun. Play might take some effort, but it always gives back. It helps you feel good. It's healthy. As you incorporate more play into your life you begin to normalize it. Eventually, you begin to see the playfulness in the mundane. You find yourself dancing in the check-out line, climbing trees, and investigating bugs. You add some flair to the kitchen as your personality starts overflowing into everything you do. You play more with your family and friends. From here, the play can even carry over into your work.

The more you play, the more fun you become. You become lighter and laugh more easily. Life becomes more pleasant.

For, when you play within all that you do, you never work again.

Chapter 6 Summary

Recap:

- No matter how you break it down, enjoyment is one of our primary purposes in human form.
- A pleasant perspective can make your day-to-day doings purely enjoyable.
- Play is part of your authentic self.
- By practicing play, or a playful perspective, you can create a habit of being in a state of play.

- Your childlike essence is still alive within you. Let it shine.

Questions to consider:

- What is your perfect form of play?
- How do you feel when you're in a state of play?
- How can you add more play to your daily life?

Challenge:

- Bring a playful perspective with you to work. Try to play while working. Be silly. Fun. Light. And, at the same time, still get your work done. At the end of the work day, reflect. How did it feel trying to incorporate play into your work? Were you successful? How was it most challenging? How did you succeed? Did it make you more effective with your work? Did it make work more enjoyable?

CHAPTER 7

Relationships

Relationships are a mirror into your being.

"Everything that irritates us about others can lead us to an understanding of ourselves."

-Carl Jung, Swiss psychiatrist and psychoanalyst

"Some of the biggest challenges in relationships come from the fact that most people enter a relationship in order to get something. They're trying to find someone who's going to make them feel good. In reality, the only way a relationship will last is if you see your relationship as a place you go to give, and not a place that you go to take."

-Anthony Robbins, American Author/Coach/Speaker

We have a variety of relationships in our life, ranging from the acquaintances we see on rare occasions to the family members we live with on a daily basis. While each of these relationships vary in their intensity and impact, each is significant in its own way.

In order to effectively examine the significance of our relationships, we'll break them out into a few categories: relationship

87

with self, relationships with others, and romantic relationships. Relationships with family will be covered in Chapter 8.

Relationship with Self

As you live, your likes and interests evolve. Your physical appearance and skill sets change. Your wisdom improves.

Yet, there are aspects of your being that always remain. There are traits you had as a child that you still have today. These traits are part of your essence. Your soul. Your true self.

One way to connect with this core aspect of yourself is through contemplation of questions related to your essence. These questions could include:

What traits did you have as a child that you still have today?

What traits have been most prominent in your best and worst of times?

Which of your likes and interests have been consistent throughout your life? What were your strengths and weaknesses as a teenager? What are your strengths and weaknesses today?

Again, which aspects of yourself have remained throughout all aspects of your journey?

The character traits that have always been with you are markers of your authentic self. They help point you toward your true essence. This person, the authentic, aligned, true essence of you, is the person you want to know better than anyone else. Once you know your essence, you are introduced to your higher self. From here, you expand and grow as you connect with the universal consciousness of love that I call Source.

But first, you need to develop a relationship with yourself. You need to learn who you are before the other magic occurs.

This goes for all aspects of your life.

In order to have effective relationships with others, you need to first have an effective relationship with yourself. In order to know others, you need to know yourself. In order to be yourself with others, you need to be yourself with yourself.

So, who are you?

I like to say that the most important thing to know is yourself.

While this sounds easy enough, many people consciously know very little about themselves. They know what's going on around the surface. They know what they do and might even have awareness around what they say. But most people don't know who they truly are. It's in them. But they haven't done the work to find it. Their authentic essence is suppressed by the requirements of life. It's been traded in for their 9-5, only to make occasional appearances on the weekend.

While this is a bleak perspective on the average relationship with oneself, it's not unrealistic. Connecting with one's essence takes work. And, this is not work that our society generally prioritizes. In return, it's work that many never do.

If, however, we develop a relationship with the essence within us -rather than ignore or deny the foundational aspects of ourselves- we can step into our authentic selves. This is a powerful self to step into.

So, let's take some time and get to know ourselves.

An easy place to start is with concrete, tangible aspects of yourself. What do you like most in the world? What makes you happiest? What do you love?

Alternatively, what bothers or upsets you? What causes pain and discord inside your body?

I recommend making a list of your "likes" and "dislikes". Listing them out about once a year is a powerful practice. Come up with as many "likes" and "dislikes" as possible. You might even want to try putting them in order of strength from your greatest "like" to your greatest "dislike".

This list starts adding color to the portrait of you.

From here, you can outline your character traits. What are your best traits? Who are you when you're most alive? What do other people love about you? What makes you different from others?

Adversely, what are your worst traits? Who are you in the face of adversity? Who are you when times are bad? What are your biggest weaknesses? What would you like to improve about yourself?

You can then reflect on who you are with the general public and who you are with your closest family members. Different people in our lives often bring out different aspects of our personality. Generally, it's those closest to us who see us at our worst.

Who are you at your worst?

Who are you at your best?

These personality traits are a big piece of the puzzle. These traits are ingrained in your essence and exist in your core. There are then additional traits ingrained in you that have been acquired from your family. Other character traits are added through the influence of your friends, media, society, and the experiences you endeavor. Your character traits -partnered with your mindset, beliefs, words, and actions- outline the painting of who you are.

After you get a clear image of your dominant character traits, you can move into developing a relationship with your motivation.

What motivates you? What inspires you?

What are your goals? Desires? Hopes and dreams?

This set of questions explains why you do the things you do.

As Simon Sinek explains in his book, "Start With Why", "regardless of WHAT we do in our lives, our WHY -our driving purpose, cause or belief- never changes."

He believes that your driving purpose always remains the same.

Your why is a part of your essence. This motivation and driving force are as deeply ingrained in your essence as your foundational character traits. It's part of who you are.

If this is an aspect of yourself you have not yet connected with, take some time to sit with it. Ask yourself why you do the things you do? Why do you have the job you have? Why do you make the money you make? Why do you care about the things you care about? As you connect with your why you will paint in more of your essence.

By answering the questions outlined above, with answers that resonate deeply within, you are provided a solid reference point for understanding who you are in physical form. With this understanding, you can work to develop a healthy relationship with the core essence of your *being*.

After this baseline understanding of self is established, it's necessary to observe your thoughts and beliefs. This brings us to your mindset.

What do you believe to be true? What do other people believe that you do not? What are your foundational morals and values? What are your thoughts on politics, religion, and Mother Earth? What do you believe in, and what do you not believe in?

These are not rhetorical questions. Rather, they are essential aspects of your being that you must develop a relationship with in order to fully embody your highest self. Sit with these questions and find answers that resonate.

From here, you can ask yourself which of your beliefs are serving you and which are not?

Unlike character traits that have more of a tendency to remain constant than change, your thoughts and beliefs generally evolve throughout your lifetime. They provide insight as to who you are today.

The more clarity you establish around your thoughts and beliefs, the better you can understand what's going on within your internal realm.

Most of the thoughts and beliefs we hold are generally acquired from our parents as we will hold the thoughts and beliefs they held until we become aware of them and work to consciously change them. We can't change thoughts and beliefs until we acknowledge them. It begins by understanding what you think and believe. From here, you can ask yourself why you hold that thought or belief.

Has it been consciously formed by life experiences, reading, and research? Or was it formed by the programming of your parents? Is the thought or belief still aligned with who you are today? Is it serving you?

Any time you find a thought or belief that is not aligned with who you are today or is not serving you, you can change it. But you can't change it until you witness it.

Your thoughts and beliefs create the reality you exist in. Choose them wisely.

The better you understand who you are today -including what you think and believe, like and dislike, want and avoid, and say and do- the healthier of a relationship you can develop with yourself. The key to developing a healthy relationship with yourself is knowing yourself. It's hard to develop a loving relationship with someone you don't know.

So what does it mean to have a healthy relationship with yourself?

It begins with understanding the foundational aspects of who you are, what you've done, and what you've experienced, and finding peace with each of them. Finding peace with your past is integrating the energy, so there is no more discord. This is to say that when you think of an event, person, or experience, from your past, you experience a positive thought or emotion. You feel good about it. You see it for what it was and are grateful.

Taking the steps to consciously observe who you are and integrate all of your discordant energy puts you in an empowered state of self-love. When you take the time to observe the inner depths of yourself, you are declaring that you care about yourself. You want to understand who you are and create the best version of yourself possible. When you do the work to integrate the discordant energy of your past, you're doubling down on this belief. This is where the rubber meets the road. Here, you make the growth real.

This is such an incredibly powerful place to be. It's a place of open-minded acceptance, radical self-discovery, and improvement.

In this place, you are declaring to the universe that you care about yourself. This energy of self-love and care will begin to radiate from you as you integrate the realities of your inner world in a way that allows your life force energy to freely flow.

This is a large part of how you develop self-love. Looking at the depths of yourself. Understanding who you are, what you think, how you act, where you show up, what you believe, and who you are at your core allows you to work on the areas where you're weak and embrace the areas in which you thrive. This honest self-reflection places you in the driver's seat for the journey ahead.

Furthermore, self-reflection is a prerequisite for self-love. Here, you can see yourself objectively, with all your beauties and flaws, your strengths and weaknesses, and your gifts and shortcomings, and embrace them all, accepting this version of yourself as being the person who you are now.

However, the person you were yesterday is not the person you need to remain today. And the person you are today is not the person you need to remain tomorrow.

As we objectively see ourselves and own our weaknesses, we are empowered to improve. When we are in a mode of denial or defense and can't see our weaknesses, it's impossible to improve upon them.

Change begins with awareness. Once we see our flaws, we can see the negative results they cause. This negativity can inspire us to change.

In this place of observing your weaknesses, seeing them, owning them, and refusing to accept them, you can begin to change them.

You are then empowered to not only improve yourself but to fall in love with the person you are, and the person you're becoming.

Love how hard you are working to improve your weaknesses. Utilize your strengths to show up in the world. Love how you show up. Love who you are in the best of times and love the effort you're putting in to improve who you are in the worst of times.

You can love every aspect of where you are on your journey when you acknowledge that it is indeed a journey.

You're doing the best you can at this time. But continue to reflect and continue to grow. When we stop reflecting and the growth halts, self-love can dissipate. Stay the course to remain filled with love.

From the space of self-love, you can treat yourself, acknowledge your accomplishments, appreciate your flaws, honor your journey, and enjoy where you are. You can love who you are, you can love the world around you, and you can love yourself.

You are allowed to love yourself.

Granted, it's hard to love yourself when you're not doing well. I've been there. It's easy to get stuck in habits of laziness, unhealthy eating, and uninspiring work. We're not always at our best. And, when we're not at our best for prolonged periods of time, it's easy to fall out of love with ourselves. We don't always love the lesser versions of ourselves. We love our potential. We love when we're inspired, and we love when we're alive.

But if we can love ourselves even when we're not at our best, then we move to a place of unconditional love.

Unconditional love. This means that you love yourself without conditions. It doesn't mean that you love yourself when you look great or are doing something you love. It means you love yourself when you raise your voice in frustration, and you love yourself when you're fired from your job. Unconditional self-love means that you love yourself no matter what because you know that you are consciously on your path doing the best you can.

This doesn't mean that you won't make mistakes. Because you will. It means that you reflect upon your mistakes and forgive yourself while making a plan to improve the mistake when moving forward. Because we all make mistakes. We all have downs. We all go through struggles. But, when you move through these spaces with unconditional self-love, you can continue to use each experience as an opportunity for continued growth and improvement to the beautiful soul you already are.

More so, we all need to give love, and we all need to receive love. Who better to give and receive love from than yourself?

Write yourself love letters. Bring yourself on dates. Enjoy time with yourself. Talk with yourself. Dance with yourself. Hug yourself. Love yourself.

As you continue to love yourself more deeply, you will not only see improvements in your personal life, but you will see improvements in your relationships with others. The more deeply you love yourself, the more deeply you can love others.

For, when you have a healthy relationship with yourself, you can embark on the journey of building healthy relationships with others.

Relationships with Others

Humans are social beings. We interact and play with others, we communicate and collaborate, we help, support, encourage, and love.

In general, we enjoy being with other people.

This most likely stems from our tribal time as we depended upon the tribe for survival. Without others, life was unsafe, scary, and dangerous. It was almost impossible to survive solo. We were dependent upon each other for survival. We taught and supported each other. We protected one another and did our part to contribute to the good of the whole.

If we didn't connect with our tribe, were ostracized for not treating others well, or did not contribute our share of work, our survival was threatened. We needed to connect with others and remain a part of the tribe if we wanted to survive.

After thousands of years of existing in tribal settings, the human desire to connect with others has been ingrained in our DNA. We've become social beings.

Today, we are not as dependent upon others for survival. We can survive fine on our own (generally after puberty) without the support of others. However, the biological desire to be with others, to be seen, supported, and appreciated, is still ingrained deep in our DNA. It's part of the human experience.

We can then take the significance of having relationships with others one step further and make the claim that we can only truly know ourselves through our interactions with others. More so, your interactions with others provide opportunities to reflect upon yourself. When you are alone, you rarely get triggered. In general, humans struggle to see what they need to work on when they're in isolation. This is part of the beauty of relationships with others.

We're thrown off center in the presence of others far more easily than when we're alone. These moments of unconscious action from a place of heightened emotions are proof that you still have work to do. Each time you are triggered, act unconsciously or respond from a place of heightened emotion, you are shown a trail head to a path that leads to work you still need to do. Your relationships with others are one of the best mirrors into your internal realms.

Our ancient ancestors generally lived in groups or tribes that were dependent upon each other for survival, yet we don't necessarily need others to survive in today's society. Survival today is easier than ever before. In return, we don't rely upon others the way we once did. It's become easy for people to get into cycles of work, sleep, repeat. We form working relationships with co-workers (and might have a family to spend some time with before bed), but today, people are existing in bubbles more than ever before. Much of today's communication even takes place behind screens rather than in person.

This has led to the suppression of our human desire to connect with -and learn from- other humans. We're isolating ourselves more and deeply connecting less.

So why, in a world where it's now easier to connect than it's ever before been, are we connecting less?

The primary answers appear to be lifestyle and education.

When we combine the pace of today's traditional lifestyle with the priority we place on working hard to hoard money, we are not left with much time to connect with others. Most people are too preoccupied with their work cycle to regularly get together with family and friends. People are comfortable in their "easy" cycles of sleep and work, which again limits connection. We have interactions with others at work but rarely deeply connect with our co-workers. We might occasionally get together with coworkers outside of work to eat a meal or have some drinks, but this is generally limited to a few hours of alcohol-induced interactions.

Much of our society will meet up with friends to enjoy food and drinks over some light hearted conversation, but we rarely meet up for the purpose of deeply connecting.

Deep connection isn't a priority in our society. We're not paid to connect with others, and we don't get any material items for connecting with others. We are a society that values money and items more than self-work and relationships.

So, we spend most of our time working hard to make money and buy things. By the time we finish our days' work, we're too tired to really connect with anyone. So, we don't. Instead, we zone out on Netflix and surf the web to distract ourselves from the work we need to do internally.

And, to be honest, we haven't really been taught to connect.

Which leads to the second reason we're lacking deep connection: education.

We are not teaching children how to effectively connect with or communicate with others. We are not developing and fostering the social skills that are necessary for us to thrive socially. Instead, our education system focuses on teaching the academic standards that students need for state tests rather than the social and emotional skills that are needed for life.

There is an art to connection that needs to be learned. Connection requires vulnerability, empathy, and communication, all skills we do not teach our youth.

This said, many people do learn how to get along with others in school. In general, school teaches us to listen and remain focused.

Schools often teach students to follow social norms and "fit in". Most people learn to make some friends in their school experience.

Unfortunately, most friendships lack true depth. Most of today's friendships primarily exist on the surface where we talk about work, shows, and the weather. We share some drinks, have some laughs, and tell some stories. We do some fun things together and we might even be there for each other in times of need.

But we rarely challenge or push each other. It's just as rare to get into philosophical debates or engage in discussions of ethics, morality, our struggles, or our real vulnerable emotions. Our friendships typically remain on the surface, focusing on all the fun things that exist on the surface: what we've listened to or watched, vacations we've enjoyed, experiences we've had, events we've gone to, etc.

It's time we add some depth to our relationships.

Start opening up and allowing yourself to be vulnerable. Share what's going on in your inner world. What are you struggling with? Where are you thriving, and where could you use support? Where are you holding yourself back? What fears do you have? What are your dreams and deepest desires? What secrets are you holding onto for only you to know?

Rather than building walls around yourself to keep others out and give you the false perception of safety, try building tables and allowing others in. Let them see the depths of yourself. Share what comes up for you. Talk about the ideas and beliefs that you're brewing. Share your sadness and your struggles, your successes and hacks.

And ask these questions of others. Hold a safe space for them to be vulnerable. Listen without judging. Empathize. If they want feedback or advice, provide it. If they need support, be there. And if they don't, keep it to yourself.

By adding these elements of connection and vulnerability to your relationships, your connections can deepen and support you in living more fully alive.

Let's examine your relationships.

The first, most important question to ask of your relationships is if they are healthy. Does the relationship add to your overall quality of life? Does the relationship make your life better or worse?

This question can be asked for all your relationships: friends, family, coworkers, acquaintances, and lovers. Ask yourself this question with all of your relationships. Is this relationship healthy? Does this relationship add to your quality of life?

Then, whenever the answer is no -this relationship is not improving your quality of life and/or is not a healthy relationship- you need to examine why.

What is your role in the relationship's struggle? Are the struggles due to something you're doing? Is there something you can do to help the relationship flourish? Generally, both parties have a responsibility when a relationship struggles. There are usually pieces for all parties to own, reflect on, learn from, and improve upon.

Some of our greatest growth can come in the face of a struggling relationship.

Through the mirror of others whom you care for and trust, you can face the reality of your true character. Relationships can reveal shadow aspects of who you've become and help you see the person you are being.

This is, if and when you honestly sit with yourself in reflection and look for it.

If you unbiasedly examine yourself (which is easier said than done) through your relationships, you can see a vision of who you are in the presence of others. You can see how you're showing up in the world.

Through this vision of yourself, you can see opportunities for growth and progress. You can make goals to improve. You can evolve and progress your internal world, which, in turn, will enhance your external world.

But growth takes work. Relationships can provide a platform for you to work from, but the relationship will not do the work. Doing the work is your responsibility.

But, if you wish to evolve into a place of *being*, you need to put in the work. You need to understand who you are, good, bad, and ugly. You need to own and accept your flaws and embrace your beauties. From here, you can improve the bad and ugly while nurturing all the good.

If, however, a relationship does not feel like it's serving you, if you are unable to see aspects of the relationship that you can improve, are unable to own your part in the relationships struggle, or are experiencing ongoing difficulty or discord on behalf of the relationship, then the relationship might be one that needs to end.

This can be tough. I've been there. But a relationship that is not serving your greatest good, that is not making your life better, and is hindering your overall quality of life, is probably a relationship that you need to move on from. We can't save all relationships.

However, there are critical steps you can take along the way to restore relationships that are taking a turn for the worse. The biggest step is looking at yourself. What is your responsibility in the relationship's struggle?

The majority of unhealthy relationships exist on a two-way street. We do things that trigger/upset the other person, which then causes them to do things that trigger/upset us. We can find ourselves in a vicious circle of sending hurtful energy back and forth to each other without a clear path to breaking the chain of cause and effect.

You can break this chain by stopping the cause and effect. You need to stop doing whatever you do that upsets the other person. Then, you need to refrain from reacting and sending it back when they trigger you.

Let's break this down further.

The first step is getting clear on whether or not this is a relationship you want to keep. If it's a relationship with someone who you respect and honor, admire and enjoy, it's a relationship you want to keep. If it's a relationship with someone who has different morals and values, or someone whose actions you don't respect, it might not be a relationship worth keeping. This could very well be why you are sending negative energy back and forth. If you want out of the relationship subconsciously but are not aware of that reality in your conscious mind, you may be passively sabotaging the relationship by reacting to things they say and do.

If there is a relationship that no longer serves you, move on from it. It does no one any good to stay in a relationship that has run its course. You need to move on when it's time to move on. Own this reality and make the change consciously. Don't let yourself subconsciously sabotage.

If, however, there's a struggling relationship that you do want to restore, you need to own your part in it. You need to see how you are showing up and observe the energy you are bringing. Are you showing up as love and sharing energy of light, or are you showing up as anger, with energy of darkness? Where on this spectrum do you lie with this relationship? How can you be more love and light?

It begins by remaining conscious. Consciously respond to your environment rather than reacting unconsciously. If negative energy is sent your way, see it, acknowledge it, maybe even honor it, and then release it. It's not yours. Let it go. Don't send it back. You alone can consciously choose to break a cycle of negativity in a relationship as it takes two people to pass negative energy back and forth. You have control over yourself and your energy. You **do not** have control over others and their energy. If they send negative energy your way, you can choose how you respond. You can choose to give them a hug, make a joke of it, or tell them that you need a break before separating yourself from the situation. These are all conscious responses that break the cycle of negative energy rather than perpetuate it.

We rarely treat others poorly consciously. It's much easier to be mean when you're acting unconsciously. More so, in a conscious state, you're aware of your actions. If you do happen to treat someone poorly, you can see it, own it, and improve it. If you're unconsciously responding, it's hard to see all the pieces that you're responsible for. It's hard to own your part and make improvements.

If you want to improve struggling relationships, you need to see your part in them, own the pieces that are yours, apologize, and work toward growth. You need to be love and light and refuse to send any negative energy their way. You must forgive them for all the wrongs you believe they've done and find peace with the past you've created together. You can then move forward aligned, in harmony and at peace.

By doing this work in your relationships, you can connect more deeply and fully. You are giving the relationship an opportunity to thrive. In doing so, you can live more fully alive.

Friendships will come and go. We grow and evolve as everyone around us does. What we need in friends at four years old is very different from what we need in friends at 24, 44 or 64 years old.

Some friendships have expiration dates as we exist in a perpetual state of change. Most friendships evolve with time. They're beautiful at their peak, as most friendships are exactly what we need at the time. Then, as we change, our friendships change with us. Some friendships weaken while others strengthen. It's part of the cycle of life. It's healthy and natural. Allow your friendships to evolve alongside you.

Let's further observe our relationships with friends.

First, we must acknowledge that we **are** in relationships with our friends. They are not generally romantic relationships, but they are relationships.

Again, the big question is whether they are healthy relationships. If they are relationships that improve your quality of life and bring enjoyment, love, or other positive emotions, then they are healthy relationships. But, if they are relationships that bring frustration, struggle, or other negative emotions, they are relationships that you might need to move on from. If the separation from a negative relationship doesn't occur naturally, you can proactively create the separation.

Hopefully, you can get to a place of having only healthy relationships.

You then need to cultivate these relationships if you want them to continue flourishing. Talk about things that matter. Be vulnerable. Discuss your thoughts and ideas. Share dreams of the future. Enjoy experiences together.

Through healthy relationships, you gain the ability to more fully experience yourself. Different aspects of who you are come out with different people. One friend may bring out your playful side, while another brings out your philosophical side. The way parts of you sync up with parts of others varies from person to person. Sometimes, you're blessed to find a friend who has all the same sides to their personality as you do. They bring out all your different sides. Other friends will only bring out some of your sides.

No matter what sides are shown, you can see yourself through others. You can see how you respond and react to what they bring, how you show up, who you are in the fun times, and who you are in the tough times.

You can grow and expand yourself in the presence of others as your energies combine to create new energetic fields. Gaining awareness of this energy is powerful. From here, you can tap into the energy and shine bright. This is just one of the many reasons why relationships are so deeply valuable.

Relationships are also fun. They're supportive. Playful. Pleasant. Interactive. Exploratory. Experiential. They provide real life learning, laughter, and enjoyment.

Relationships are beautiful in so many ways.

Good friends can be real and honest with us in ways that are hard for others. They can help us see our strengths and flaws, our gifts and weaknesses. They can help us when climbing up and support us when sinking down. They can provide insight and perspective, knowledge and skill. They can model traits and behaviors that we're still working on and inspire us to be better versions of ourselves.

Friends can be fun and helpful, supportive and enjoyable. They make us feel good. Friends make life better.

But friendships also require work.

In order to have healthy relationships with friends, we need to do our part. We need to be there for them when we are needed and support them as necessary. We need to show up and contribute our beautiful self so that they can show up and contribute their beautiful selves. We get out what we put in.

Sometimes, you might have a friend in need as our friends go through tough times too. Being there for them through these times is an opportunity to serve. This is ultimately beneficial for both you and them. Yet, supporting them might become challenging. They might even get stuck and resist your support. In these times, you can practice empathy and grace. Do what you can, and know that the work is still on them. You can be there for them, but you can't do the work for them.

Friendships give us an opportunity to show up for people. They provide practice in giving and caring. Friendships help us and support us on our journey through life.

Together, in healthy friendships, we can expand to become even more beautiful both as individuals and as friends.

While all the relationships in your life are significant in their own ways, the relationship with your lover is unique to itself. We've built a society that's primarily monogamous, leading most people to experience the beauty of sexuality with one person at a time. Sexual relationships are powerful and intense and fall into a category of their own.

For, when we are intimate sexually, we have the opportunity to be alive in our purest form. There is no clothing hiding us, no tv distracting us, and no work bothering us. We can simply be alive, in the present moment, connecting with our partner. In this space, we can feel every sensation and hear every sound. Here, we are freed from worries of what we have to do tomorrow or resentment toward what happened yesterday.

Sexuality can bring us into the present moment in a way that little else can. It's a pathway into our body, allowing us to feel deeply while potentially experiencing bliss. It can unite two souls while supporting them to drop into a vast expanse of beingness.

Through these beautiful aspects of sexuality, we become connected. We develop emotions toward those we are intimate with, and we allow ourselves to be vulnerable. Sex is vulnerable. Our sexual partner sees us in our rawest form, a form we allow few people to see us in. By allowing our sexual partners to see us in this raw, vulnerable form, they experience the best and the worst we have to offer.

Over time, they begin to see our true being. We generally give our lovers the opportunity to see us more fully than anyone else. Ideally, we are honestly real with them in a way that allows them to see all of us. Good, bad, and ugly. Strengths and weaknesses. Gifts and struggles. Beauties and flaws. They have the opportunity to truly see who we are. They can see us fully. All of us.

Through their knowingness of who we are, we can work with their insight and perspective to gain a deeper understanding of who we're being. Real, raw conversations with our lovers, about the essence of who we are, can be profoundly insightful. They can illuminate blind spots that are difficult to see, provide perspective on where you're thriving and struggling, and invoke understanding of your ultimate essence. Through partnership, you can paint a more vividly complete image of the person you are being than you can independently.

In addition to all the other beautiful roles your lover can play, they are often your greatest teacher (though children and parents are right there as well). By remaining aware of how you show up with them and how you respond (or occasionally react) to the life you experience together, you are given a mirror to see yourself.

Through every interaction, reaction, response, and emotion you feel with your partner, you are shown an aspect of your being.

For, when you are triggered or feel an emotional response to something they say or do, it provides an opportunity to look within and observe why you were triggered. Why were you affected the way you were, and why did you respond the way you did? At the root of these answers lies the opportunity for great growth.

When your lover has a problem with something you say or do, there is an aspect of the problem that is on them, but an equal amount of the problem that is on you. They are allowing your actions to affect them, which is a choice they are making, but at the same time, you are responsible for your actions.

If you are doing things that hurt others, you need to change the things you're doing. You need to reflect upon your actions and acknowledge the way you're being. This is an opportunity to see your flaws and own the times when you don't act in integrity with your highest self. From here, you can create a plan and take inspired action to improve yourself. This process can become a catalyst for your growth and development.

As you grow and develop, you move closer to existing in a perpetual state of being fully alive.

In healthy intimate relationships, you can show up authentic, vulnerable, and real. You can express yourself and be yourself more deeply and fully than you can independently. Healthy sexual relationships make life more complete and whole.

Yes, we are already complete and whole individually, but partnership allows us to experience other aspects of life that we cannot experience on our own. In this way, partnerships make life even more complete and whole.

Intimate relationships provide an opportunity to experience a greater range of emotions as you can feel both your emotions and your partner's emotions. And sometimes, your emotions can overlap and interconnect to create super emotions. Super emotions can be beautiful, light, and inspiring, or heavy, dark, and difficult. Either way, they are full expressions of the human experience. These full experiences expand our boundaries. They provide perspective and teach us lessons. They help us live more fully alive.

While on the topic of intimate relationships, I'd also like to touch on sexual energy.

Sexual energy is a powerful life force that is generally undervalued. We live in a world that bombards us with sexual images and ideas while shying away from real conversations on sexuality and sexual energy. In return, many humans never learn to develop a healthy relationship with their sexual energy. Instead, it remains a driving force at the core of many actions and decisions that we barely understand. While this leads some to promiscuous lives of random hook ups, it creates sexual frustration in others. This sexual frustration is then released through masturbation, pornography, or other low vibrational releases, that do not move us toward a high vibrational state of *being*.

If, however, our sexual energy is harnessed and directed, it can become an incredibly powerful tool. If we learn to work with it rather than against it, our sexual energy can uplift and inspire us.

Unfortunately, this is not the norm in today's society, as we're not talking openly and candidly about sexuality or sexual energy. There's still taboo around it.

This is partially due to the negative sexual energy that's infiltrating our planet. Sex trafficking. Priests and children. Powerful executives on sex islands. These are manifestations of our unhealthy sexual energy.

Sexuality needs to be discussed.

We can start with porn.

I recommend going a month without it. Check in on how you feel throughout the month. It might be hard at first, but how do you feel at the back end of the month? Have you been more productive than you were while watching porn? Have your energy levels been more consistent?

Try to transmute your sexual energy. Rather than expelling it to porn, try channeling it toward healthy pursuits. Allow your sexual energy to flow through you, fill you with happiness, release it into the world through positive thought, and breathe it back in. Feel your sexual energy not just through orgasms but through your existence on a moment-to-moment basis. Sexual energy is an energy of passion and life. It's full of love and happiness. It's powerful energy! Harness it. Embrace it. Stop releasing it to low vibrational pictures and allow it to lift you up to a higher state of being.

A concrete way to experience the power of sexual energy is through the practice of tantric sex. One specific aspect of tantra that's directly tied to your ability to feel the sexual energy is breath. Breathing.

I recommend getting in the yab yum (lotus) position, where one partner sits on top of the other partner's lap. Sync up your breathing, so you are both taking 5 second inhales through your nose together, then exhaling through your mouth for 5 seconds. Settle into the rhythm of this breath together. Deep inhale, deep exhale. Slow your breathing.

After being inside each other for 10 or 20 conscious breaths, you should begin to feel the energetic field in and around you begin to multiply. The energy will begin to rise up through you with a radical intensity. Feel the energy in and around you. Feel how powerful this energy is. Feel its unlimited abundance. Feel it's love and radiance. Stay in this place. Tantric sex doesn't have the goal of orgasm; rather, the goal is deep connection. Feel this connection. Feel the energy between you. Absorb it. Bask in it. Play with it.

Sexual energy is one of the most powerful energies we have on our planet. Rather than succumbing to the belief that your sexual energy is too strong and you need to release it to remain pleasant and chill, try holding the energy. It takes some practice as it is indeed a lot of energy, but it's not too much. You can not only learn to embrace this energy, but to hold, harness, and focus it.

Masturbation is the opposite of holding, harnessing, and focusing your sexual energy. Masturbation is releasing the energy.

Learning to harness and control your sexual energy can benefit you in multiple areas of life. It frees you from the perpetual desire for sex. It increases your energy levels and many studies say it improves your creativity. More importantly, it gives you control over your energy. When you take control of your sexual energy you can use it in ways that serve you. When you are enslaved to your sexual energy, it will use you.

Harness your sexual energy, absorb its power, and become even more fully alive.

Chapter 7 Summary

Recap:

- You need to develop a healthy relationship with your authentic self before you can develop a healthy and authentic relationship with someone else.
- Work to understand and outline the full range of thoughts, feelings, emotions, traits, genes, stories, and beliefs that make you.
- Declare to the universe that you love yourself and fill your cup with self-love.
- We have an inherent desire to connect and form relationships with others.
- You can greater see yourself through your relationships with others.
- You do not have control over other people or their energy.
- Form healthy relationships that serve you.

Questions to consider:

- Who are you?
- What beliefs do you hold that serve you? Which of your beliefs do not serve you?
- What do you love about yourself? How can you love yourself more?
- What positives do you bring to your relationships? What negatives do you bring?

Challenge:

- Create a list of as many things you love about yourself as possible. Try to get at least 100. As you write each thing you love about yourself, feel gratitude and appreciation for that aspect of yourself. What do you not love about yourself? Why do you not love these aspects of you? What can you do to shift these aspects and love them more?

Next Level Challenge:

- Practice harnessing your sexual energy. Take a break from porn. Masterbate on occasion, bringing yourself 75% of the way to climax, then stop. Feel the sexual energy alive in you. Let it flow through your chakras and permeate your field. Then, focus this energy on a dream or goal. After practicing to hold this energy for a few days (or ideally a few weeks), and you finally do reach orgasm, focus the life force energy of the orgasm toward your dream or goal. Watch it manifest itself in reality.

CHAPTER 8

Family

Family can be your greatest teacher.
Allow them to teach you.

"Home is where you are loved the most and act the worst."
-Marjorie Pay Hinckley, American religious leader and author

"There is no doubt that it is around the family and the home that all the greatest virtues, the most dominating virtues of humans, are created, strengthened and maintained."
-Winston Churchill, Prime Minister of the United Kingdom from 1940-1945 and 1951-1955

Living with the same people day in and day out, year after year, creates deep emotions. We experience the cycle of life and death with family. We celebrate life's highs and endure life's struggles. We laugh, and we cry. We talk, and we play. We teach each other, and we grow together. As difficult as aspects of family can be, family provides some of our greatest memories and fondest experiences.

These experiences are polarizing. We love our family in a way that is unique to family. At the same time, we get frustrated and triggered by family in a way that is equally unique. Siblings get angry with each other and fight in ways they never would with others. There are sides of us that come out with family that don't come out elsewhere. Families challenge each other. They push each other to grow. We know the strengths and weaknesses of our family members, how to push their buttons, and how to laugh and have fun with them.

This all combines in a way that makes family another great teacher.

Family is a mirror. When you're good and balanced, things are good with family. When you're off, your family life is generally off. Therefore, when there's a problem with your spouse, child, parent, or sibling, you can look inward. What are you doing that is causing these issues? What part of this discord is your responsibility? What can you do to change it?

Because, although you can't change others, you can change yourself. As much as you may want to help those you love to grow and evolve, you must accept that you can't change anyone other than yourself.

What you can do is make the improvements you can on your end while finding peace with the pieces that are theirs. From here, you can laugh at their idiosyncrasies and smile at their beauties. You can embrace their flaws and love them as whole, complete people.

What you cannot do is change their weaknesses. If you have a problem with an aspect of someone else, you really have a problem with yourself. This is **your** problem with them. It's a problem you are creating, around an aspect of them, that triggers something in you.

If they had a problem with themselves, they would probably fix it. If you're bothered by something they do, you can share your feelings and speak your truth, but you can't change them.

You can, however, change the story you're telling yourself about them.

Or, more importantly, you can resolve the problem within yourself, so you are no longer triggered by them.

Every argument we have, every disagreement, complaint, dislike, or issue we have with someone else, generally reflects a problem we have with ourselves. For, when we observe another, without judgment, we see they have nothing wrong. They are exactly as they are.

Yet, we are plagued with the disease of holding resentment, animosity, or other negative thoughts and feelings toward others. Sometimes, people hold this negativity for years. Other times, we create negative stories about people we haven't even met. More often than not, the negative thoughts and feelings we hold toward others are stories we have created. Fortunately, stories can be rewritten. Suppose you once wrote a negative story about someone because you were hurt or upset. In that case, you can later rewrite the story from a positive perspective.

Because everyone is on their own individual journey, just like you and me. We all have our issues and struggles we are working through. We have our strengths and weaknesses, some of which we are conscious of, others which may exist within our shadows.

Yet, no matter where you are in your individual journey, family remains a mirror to reflect on yourself.

Family carries emotional connections and ties, biological alignment, and history that roots back to your first day in this life. We might even span other lifetimes and alternative realms together. The connection we feel with family is often one of the strongest bonds we experience in physical form. Family allows us to challenge and push each other, love and support each other, and provide opportunities to develop and grow.

My Mom is a great woman with a huge heart. She was a stay at home Mom through my childhood, always bringing my siblings and I camping, building and creating with us, and supporting us in everything we wanted to try. She instilled strong morals and values and has a deep connection to the spiritual realms. And, like everyone, she has her demons. She's had an incredibly challenging life and has integrated pieces of her journey while still struggling with others.

I've had my difficulties with her. I've seen her pains and her flaws. I see them in her and I see them in myself. Some of her flaws used to drive me crazy. I've always loved her deeply, but she was challenging for me at times because I cared for her and wanted her to grow. In return, I always pointed out her flaws. I'd point out her raised voice and intense energy. I'd make passive aggressive comments about the messes around the house and her critical nature. I wanted her to be aware of these issues. I tried giving advice and recommendations. I gave her books to read and songs to listen to. But little of it helped. It was not my place to "fix" her.

It was not until I began to detach from her flaws -through meditation and perspective- that we were able to improve our relationship. I needed to appreciate who she was and stop seeing who she was not. More importantly, I needed to look at myself. Why was I being affected by her? Why was I so emotional around her? Why would I allow her to trigger me? Why did her words negatively affect me?

The answer to most of these questions pointed right back at myself. Her flaws triggered me because I had the same flaws. I was frustrated with these traits in her because I was frustrated with these traits in myself.

I then went through a similar process in learning to fully see and appreciate my sisters and then, my wife.

My daughters will continue to show me my work for years to come.

Family has a way of doing this. As I stated earlier, family can be our greatest teacher. We spend more time with family than anyone else. They get to know us better than anyone, and we get to know them better than anyone. This can lead to a lot of emotions. Our work is to understand the emotions, integrate the negative ones, and harness the positive ones.

You can do so by being non-judgemental, unbiased, and detached from the flaws of your family members. Focus on the positives. See them for the beautiful people they are. Acknowledge the traits that you love.

More importantly, to maintain positive relationships, work on yourself. Gain awareness around your triggers. Understand why others trigger you. Use this trigger to look within. Allow yourself to heal the issue. Move toward existing as a family in love.

For, when you live in love with your family, you can more effectively live fully alive, in love with yourself.

While most human beings are blessed to be born into families that love them, this is not the case for everyone. There are children born to parents who don't know how to love, while others are born to biological parents who are not ready to have them. In some cases, the child is put up for adoption in hopes of finding parents who are capable of loving and supporting them. In these cases, the child might live in the foster care system for months, or even years, before experiencing the love of family.

Other times, people move away from their families for one reason or another. Many of our ancestors traveled across the ocean, never to return to their families in hope of creating a better life.

Sometimes, family members die; other times, they change to reject their family.

In each of these cases, an individual can be left without family to fall back on when the challenges of life appear.

Others grow to become very different from their family. They continue evolving and progressing as their family remains stagnant. Morals and values change and they grow apart.

Fortunately, we do not need to be connected by blood to be family. I've been blessed with an amazing biological family that I love unconditionally. My sisters are two of my favorite people in the world. My cousins are like brothers and I adore my Aunts and Uncles. Yet, I moved about 3000 miles away from them while working to find myself in my 20's. In order to find who I was, I had to move away from the influence of my family.

With time, I made new friends. As life progressed, we grew closer. We had deep meaningful conversations, new experiences, and some good ol' fashion fun. We pushed each other to grow. We supported each other and held each other accountable. Eventually, they started to feel like brothers.

We occasionally push each other's buttons like brothers may do, but at the same time, we love each other like brothers do. We are there for each other, we celebrate holidays and major life events, and at times, have even lived together.

Through these experiences, I've acknowledged that we don't need to be related by blood to be family. Family is a feeling of being loved and accepted for exactly who we are. It's knowing that those people will be there for you no matter what. They love you unconditionally.

These aspects of family are more important than shared blood. It's the love that makes the family. Not the blood. Follow the love, and keep finding your family.

They say you can't love another until you love yourself. Which, in many cases, is true. But it's not necessarily true in regard to family. With family, we often love unconditionally. When a parent has a child, there is naturally a deep and profound love. When a big sister meets her sibling, there is natural love. That said, family can put us in a situation where we unconditionally love another, despite what we think of ourselves.

Yet, if we do not know how to love ourselves, it can become increasingly difficult to love others. The inherent love that we can feel as children will fade if we do not nurture it. We need to practice having a positive relationship with ourselves. Because all relationships take effort. We need to put effort into our relationship with ourself, and we need to put effort into our relationships with others.

The effort you put into yourself is primarily based around doing your personal work. Doing your work includes developing an understanding of who you are and who you want to be. It's acknowledging your strengths and weaknesses and consciously working to improve them. It's forgiving yourself for the wrongs you've done and the pain you've caused. It's healing your traumas and finding peace with your past.

This work takes time and effort. Healing yourself is real work. But it's some of the most important work there is to do.

For, once you reach a place of complete and unwavering peace of your past, you can become fully alive in the present.

Being fully alive in the present allows you to make the effort needed for your relationships to thrive. It's hard to put the effort into the present when you're still living with pain or frustration from the past. The past needs to be cleared… as difficult as that may be.

For, after the past is at peace, and you are alive in the present, you can begin to thrive in all aspects of life.

One of these primary aspects you can thrive in is your relationships. In order to make relationships work, you need to put in effort. The effort aspect of relationships generally takes on three primary forms: interest, investment, and involvement.

Being involved is knowing what they are up to and being involved in it. Do things together. Connect. Play. Talk about what's going on in life. What are they excited about? What are they working on? What are they struggling with? What are their goals?

Being involved means that you engage in their life. You do things together. Share experiences. Reflect. Hang and chat. Help them out. Be there. Listen. Share. Support. Connect. Play.

Being interested grows from the involvement. We become interested in what's going on with them (and care) which makes us invested. Being invested means that you care. When you have an emotional connection to someone, you grow invested. You care how they're doing and will do what you can to help them as needed.

Being interested is wondering and caring about someone. When they talk and engage with you, you have an opportunity to be interested. This can be demonstrated by asking follow-up questions or asking about other aspects of their lives that you find interesting. How has so-and-so been? What's going on with your thingamajig? These can be fun and light check-ins or deep and philosophical conversations. Either way, it cultivates your relationship. Being interested is being a good friend and a good family member.

Now, like anything, being a good friend needs to be natural. If you run through a script of interview type questions in order to connect with someone, it's going to be awkward. You're not being interested, invested, or involved. Being interested involves sincere care. When you sincerely care, it's authentic. When it's authentic, the interest is real.

However, simply being interested, invested, and involved, does not make a relationship healthy. Healthy relationships are based on the person you are when you're with them and the way that you feel around them. Are you being a great version of yourself when you are with this person? Do you feel great when you are with this person? If either of these answers are no, then I recommend looking at the why. Why are you not being a great version of yourself in this relationship? Why do you not feel great when you're with this person? After finding these answers, you can either begin working to change the habits and patterns of the relationships or, if necessary, you can end the relationship. Those are the two primary options, as maintaining the status quo in an unhealthy relationship should not be an option.

Our relationships should build us up and improve our quality of life. If they are not for the better, they need to change.

One final aspect of being with family which I'd like to touch upon is children.

Having children is magical on many levels, but one of the greatest aspects of *being* a parent is how effective our children can teach us to *be*.

Children are fully present. Always. Trying to do something else while hanging out with a toddler is almost impossible. Being with children is a great practice in *being*. They walk slowly, looking at the world through a fresh perspective. Walks with children are not an attempt to get from one location to the next effectively or efficiently. Rather, they are a timeless wander of magical possibility.

This is how children approach everything they do. They are fully immersed, alive and excited, with passion and emotion, 100% alive in the moment.

It's unbelievably refreshing to be in the presence of this much presence.

And it can be equally difficult. It can challenge you on so many levels. Having children is entirely selfless. They don't care how little sleep you've had or what's going on with your emotions. They want you fully present with them, no matter what. Children teach us lessons that are hard to otherwise learn. They teach us to slow down, look at the flowers, awe at the bugs, be imaginative, and love unconditionally. They are incredible teachers. They are pure love and light and are one of the greatest gifts of human form.

There is so much to learn from a child's full body presence and awareness. They feel fully. They engage fully. They are in the moment, fully. While they may not always have the words to effectively convey what they are feeling, they are always feeling. They think and wonder. They question the world around them and are regularly filled with awe of it.

While these traits are so prominent in children, they often dissipate as we are conditioned by society. As a parent, or as an adult in a child's life (aunt, uncle, teacher, sitter, etc.), we have an opportunity to not only support our children in further developing and grasping hold of these pure traits but to learn from them on our journey to re-embody these traits that many adults have struggled to maintain.

Of all the incredible teachers I've had the privilege of working with, my daughters are two of the greatest teachers I've found. When they are upset, I try to look within and ask myself what role I have in their emotions. When they behave in a manner I don't appreciate, I ask myself how I've helped create that behavior. When they say something I'm not a fan of, I ask how I've contributed to that thought or belief.

After going in to sit with myself and these questions, I create a plan of inspired action to help me evolve as a better parent. Through this practice, I've learned as much about myself through my daughters as I have through any teacher, book, class, or experience I've found.

While having children is definitely not for everyone, it can be profoundly impactful in tangible ways. It's not easy. And it's definitely a lot of work. But I struggle to find work as significant, insightful, helpful, or as meaningful as raising children. For those who do choose to experience this life changing endeavor, I wish you peace and clarity in learning the lessons they present and enjoying the beauty of Being that children bring.

Chapter 8 Summary

Recap:

- Everything about your family members that is difficult for you, or bothers you, is an opportunity to explore yourself.
- Focus on the positives in people. See them for the beautiful, full people who they are, not who they are not.
- While some love is unconditional, all relationships need nurturing.
- Be interested, involved, and invested in your relationships.
- Learn from the awareness and presence of children.

Questions to consider:

- Why is that way about your family member difficult for you? How can you learn and grow from it?

- How do you nurture your relationships? Which of your relationships need nurturing? How can you provide it?
- When have you seen a child fully present and aware? What were they doing? What can you learn from it?

Challenge:

- Select a relationship with a family member that could be improved. Then, find a reason why you would like to deepen this relationship. What can/will you do to improve the relationship? Do it. Sit down and have a real heart to heart conversation with them. Reflect on the conversation. Improve the parts that are yours and release the parts that are theirs.

CHAPTER 9

Being Physical

*You are a physical being.
Align your physical body with your mental,
emotional, and spiritual bodies to live fully alive.*

"Your physical self is inspired by a divine force that beats its heart, digests its food and grows its fingernails, and this same force is receptive to endlessly abundant health."

-Wayne Dyer, American self-help and spiritual author and motivational speaker

"Spirit is the life, the mind the builder, the physical the result."

-Edgar Cayce, American clairevoyant

You are a complex being that exists in the mental, emotional, spiritual, and physical realms. Let's observe the physical aspects of *being*.

Here, in the Earthly plane, the physical body links your mental, emotional and spiritual bodies. Your meat suit is the vehicle through which you explore and enjoy the Earthly experience. As you optimize your physical being, new options and opportunities will unlock themselves in the physical world. For, in the Earthly realm, your physical body is the vehicle in which you get to enjoy your journey.

If we go back to examine our tribal selves, we see that being physical was required for survival. We walked a lot. We carried water and wood and everything else that needed to be moved. We hunted and gathered. Sometimes we fought. Early in our development, we were primarily in our physical body as survival required physical work and labor.

As we've evolved, our survival has become far less dependent upon our physical bodies. We've adapted to the changes in our environment, our minds, and every other change that's been thrown at us. We're incredibly adaptable. We've had to be. Either adapt, or die. When we needed to walk 20 miles a day for months on end, we did so. And, when we gained the ability to stay at home working on a computer, again, we adapted.

Unfortunately, not all of these changes have been beneficial to our health. We are now living the most stationary life we've ever lived. In return, we're seeing a prevalence of type 2 diabetes and obesity in our culture that we've never before seen. You can now survive without being in shape physically. However, there's a big difference between surviving and thriving. It's hard to fully thrive when your physical body is struggling.

We can still sit at a computer, eat a meal, and watch some shows when we're not doing well physically, but it's hard to hike a mountain, swim in the waves, or dance along to the music of life. The greater physical health we have, the more fully we can live.

With the physical body serving as the vehicle through which you experience life in the Earthly realm, many of the fullest experiences in life are physical. Dancing. Sex. Climbing trees and jumping in leaves. When we're fully engaged physically, it often puts us in the present moment with complete awareness. In this place, endorphins are released, adrenaline can be activated, awareness is heightened, presence becomes complete, and we become filled. It's fulfilling to use your physical body. It wants to be used.

The body wants to move freely and express itself. It has an innate desire to climb, dance, run, and play. We've been using the body in these ways since our earliest days and still desire them today.

One of the most direct portals we have to experience the immersive awareness of being fully alive is using the body in a way that allows the mind and soul to unite in pure presence. Sex often brings us to this place. Dancing does it. We can get there through running, surfing, skating, riding, skiing, and hiking. Playing games. Maybe gardening, writing, creating art, or playing music. These are all forms of using the body to align the mind and soul to be purely present in the moment. In this place, everything is heightened. Here, we experience life more fully than we do in our resting state.

These physical activities and experiences are all aspects of the full human experience.

Using the physical body must be part of the equation to living fully alive. You don't need to use your body fully every day, but it does need to be part of your lifestyle.

Unfortunately, as society shifts to being more technology based, where people work remotely over a computer, we are seeing less physical activity than ever before. The hunter/gatherer version of ourselves was believed to walk around 6 miles per day whereas the Mayo Clinic says Americans now walk an average of around 2 miles per day. Our society has evolved in a way that requires us to walk less.

Many people no longer "need" to use their bodies. So, they don't. They work from a computer, drive to their destinations, and have their needs brought to them.

However, just because you don't "need" to use your body to survive, you do need to use your body to thrive.

When we become sedentary, our systems struggle. A team of Australian researchers surveyed more than 3.300 government employees and found that men who sat for more than 6 hours a day were 90 percent more likely to feel moderate psychological distress- like feeling nervous, restless, hopeless, or tired- than men who sat for less than 3 hours a day.

We've also found that our mind is more healthy and stays sharp longer, in people who are physically active and healthy, than people who are not.

Then there's the endorphins that are released when we exercise, which make us feel good.

Not to mention the increased energy and motivation that we find in those who are physically active.

In looking at the research, it becomes increasingly apparent that being active is an integral aspect of our ability to thrive. Our body optimizes itself when active. It diminishes when inactive.

If you want your brain to be fully turned on, your energy levels to be high, your endorphins to be released, and your stoke to be activated, you need to use your body.

The stoke is a powerful experience. When stoked, you're fully alive. Your senses are heightened, excitement and energy are high, bliss is present, you're stimulated and motivated, engaged, present, and aware.

It's that feeling of, "Woooooo! Duuuuudeee!!".

Some adrenaline might be released. Your blood is pumping, and your heart is beating. You feel big feelings as your senses become heightened. Your body is activated, turned on, allowing energy to flow through you. The stoke is a feeling of being fully alive.

The stoke is a portal to being fully alive that anyone can experience. It might not be a preferred portal for the timid, nervous, or cautious types, but even these personality traits have the ability to step out of their comfort zone to expand themselves and experience the feeling of being fully alive in stoke.

I started skiing at 5 years old and was introduced to the stoke shortly thereafter. Skiing gave me the feeling of flying. I felt connected to myself and the environment. I was in my body, fully alive.

I still access the stoke through skiing to this day.

I then experienced it through scoring touchdowns and crushing baseballs. I found it while performing on the stage and building new creations. A little later in life, I found a similar stoke when I started kissing girls and summiting mountains. I've experienced it while dancing and playing music. Most recently, I found the stoke through surfing.

One of the biggest common threads amongst all these versions of stoke is the element of stepping outside of your comfort zone.

Stepping outside of your comfort zone also happens to be a critical aspect of living fully alive. Let's observe the comfort zone.

The comfort zone is a place where you are safe and protected. You can predict the environment and generally know what to expect. In the comfort zone, you have an element of control around the experience. There's generally some consistency or sameness. Most of our daily tasks, work, and pleasure exist within the comfort zone.

In the comfort zone, there's little risk or danger. It's safe, predictable, and reliable. It can be nurturing, kind, and comforting.

Although the comfort zone can be an easy place to live, growth doesn't occur in the comfort zone. In order to experience growth, we need to step outside of our comfort zone and into our growth zone.

The growth zone is the area outside of the comfort zone where you are stepping into the unknown. New environments, experiences, and activities are generally located in the growth zone. You don't know what to expect or what's going to happen in this place. You are stretched. You might be slightly uncomfortable, unsure, or unprepared. It can be scary.

However, the more you step out of the comfort zone and into the growth zone, the more your comfort zone expands. The more you expand. As you sit in new environments and situations, you eventually become comfortable in them. The edge of your comfort zone expands to include areas that were previously in your growth zone. You become more well-rounded, more comfortable, and more versed. You expand and become more full.

The outer edge of your comfort zone (inner edge of your growth zone) is a beautiful place to be. It's the place where you are slightly uncomfortable, forcing yourself to stretch and grow.

However, if you step too far outside of your growth zone, you begin to reach your danger zone. Here, it's too scary. You begin to shut down and protect yourself. You can't grow here. It's too much.

The key is finding the goldilocks zone, between your comfort zone and your danger zone, where you can endure new experiences, push yourself, and expand. The more time you spend here, the further your growth zone expands. Eventually, you develop the tools and skills necessary to transform the area that was once a danger zone, into a growth zone.

As these zones continue to expand, you continue to grow. You become more full, gaining the ability to thrive in more situations and environments.

Kids provide a great lens to observe these zones through. They are generally fully alive in their house with their parents, talking, laughing and playing. You see their personality on full display as they are safe and free to simply *be*.

When they go out to a new environment, maybe a new friend's house or a park, they stay close to their parents at first. They don't say much and are nervous to explore or engage. The parents provide comfort in this environment as the children expand their comfort zone. As some time passes, they begin feeling more comfortable. They start to wander farther from their parents and engage more fully. Eventually, they start to laugh and play. Their personality begins to shine, and once again, they are fully alive.

But if the environment is too much, they shut down. They cry and want to be held. In this place, they can't expand their comfort zone.

The more children step into new environments, the greater their comfort zone expands. Eventually, these environments become comfortable, and the transition period of hanging by their parents' side dissipates.

This is the same for adults. The more we step into new environments, the more comfortable we become. The more we push ourselves outside of our comfort zone, to a space that is slightly uncomfortable, the more tools and skills we gain to exist within that environment.

I've been playing music since my early 20's. Yet, playing with others, and playing in front of others has remained at the edge of my growth zone, bordering on the danger zone. It was so scary.

When I tried, I'd get all tight, and start to shut down. My heart would race, I felt butterflies in my stomach, and I got totally in my head. I was in a place of fight or flight. So I fled. I continued to shy away from playing music around others as it scared me.

But I'd play around my daughters, which felt really good. This gave me the confidence to play in front of my students. I then started to play with some friends. Slowly, it became more comfortable. What was once the edge of my danger zone was slowly working its way into my comfort zone. Playing music has been a long journey for me. It's still not fully within my comfort zone, but I now love playing with others. And, every time I do so, I feel myself becoming more comfortable with it. Eventually, playing music with and in front of others will be fully within my comfort zone.

As we continue to step into spaces that are uncomfortable, spaces within our growth zone, they become more comfortable.

Eventually, you can get to a place where you can go wherever you want, try whatever you are called to, and explore all aspects of the human experience, without experiencing the shut-down of the danger zone.

Again, this is a beautiful place to be.

By expanding your comfort zone to include more and more of the full human experience, you give yourself the ability to endure more of the full human experience. You grow. You expand. Life becomes more full.

While many of the fullest life experiences are physical, there are other experiences that are mental, emotional, or spiritual. For many people, the path to experiencing the full range of mental, emotional, and spiritual experiences begins with expanding yourself physically. As physical beings in a physical world, this is the most tangible realm for us to exist in.

If jumping off the 40-foot cliff at the Venus Pools on the road to Hana is too much for you, walk down to the 20-foot section. If this is still in your danger zone, go down to the 10-foot drop. Your heart may be racing as you look down to the water below. Your nerves might activate as you experience a feeling of nervous excitement. Take some deep breaths, control your breathing, and have faith in yourself. Take the leap. As you fly toward the water, feel the life pumping through you. As you're submerged in the water, floating toward the surface, feel the excitement of stepping outside your comfort zone. As you surface, let the adrenaline, joy, and stoke wash over you. Smile. Laugh. Let the excitement flow. Embrace it. Then, take the stoke with you as inspiration to continue stepping outside your comfort zone. Go try the rope swing. Summit the mountain. Get on the dance floor. Join in the game.

As you expand physically, take the stoke with you to expand in other realms. Talk with the homeless man then pitch your business to the multi-millionaire. Engage with the crush who's out of your league. Discuss sex and religion. Try psychedelics and plant medicines. All of them. Visit third world countries. Go fast in the woods. Adventure into nature alone, without a plan for where you'll sleep. Eye gaze. Connect deeply and vulnerably. Share your secrets. Explore the depths of your psyche. And as you do so, continue to feel the excitement of watching your comfort zone expand and grow.

We then have the lifestyle aspect of our physical being. Much of the developed world has created a lifestyle based on working desk jobs, sitting in front of screens, and pressing repeat. Some people go to the gym a few times a week, and we have sex, but most people don't too much physical activity outside of that.

We're trying to fit healthy activities into our lifestyle rather than create a healthy lifestyle.

There are so many little things we can do to bring our physical body into our lifestyle.

I haven't been to the gym in over 20 years yet I'm in the best shape of my life. I do some yoga and meditation every day, and my age in push-ups. I started doing the push-ups in my early 30's. When I turned 35, I'd do 35 push-ups a day. I'm now doing over 40 a day. I look forward to keeping it going into my 100's.

Outside of yoga and push-ups, I don't have any other daily workouts. But I love to surf and ski and do them a few times a month. I play with my kids. I dig in the garden and do work around the yard. I build things out of wood. I go for walks and hikes. I dance when I feel a beat. I have sex. These are all activities which not only bring me enjoyment but lead to increased physical health.

I've developed hobbies and habits that I absolutely love, that bring me into my body and allow me to experience the physical aspect of *being*.

From here, when we're grounded in our physical body, strongly and confidently, we can more easily access our emotional and spiritual bodies. They're all connected. When we're not grounded in our physical body it can be difficult to embrace our emotional and spiritual bodies. It's not impossible, but it is more difficult. The physical body is more concrete and easy to access than the emotional and spiritual bodies. Therefore, it's often the most effective path into our other bodies.

Find the physical activities that you love. Use them to get into your body as you continue to connect more deeply with yourself.

Chapter 9 Summary

Recap:

- Your physical body is the vehicle in which you get to enjoy the human experience.
- It's hard to fully thrive when your physical body is struggling.
- Through the use of the physical body, your mind and soul can unite in a way that brings deep presence and awareness.
- The benefits of being physically active are vast. Some primary benefits include release of endorphins,

increased mental health, improved energy, and a stoked type bliss.

- Step out of your comfort zone and into your growth zone to expand and evolve.
- Create a physically active lifestyle instead of trying to fit physical activity into your lifestyle.

Questions to consider:

- How is your physical body thriving? How does your physical body struggle?
- What's one specific action item you can take on to improve your physical health?
- When do you feel the best in your physical body? When do you feel the most presence and awareness?

Challenge:

- Step outside of your comfort zone and into your growth zone. Think of something you want to do but have had reservations or fear around. Push yourself to have this experience. Get up on the stage and perform your song. Talk to the crush who's out of your league. Learn the new skill that scares you. After stepping out of your comfort zone and experiencing the growth zone, reflect on the experience. How did it feel being in the growth zone? How did you expand and/or grow? How did this experience benefit you? How else can you step out of your comfort zone? Find ways to continue experiencing the beauty of the growth zone.

Being Healthy

Your life force is tied to your health.
Optimize your health and increase your life force.

"Let food be thy medicine and medicine be thy food."

-Hippocrates, Greek physician considered
"Father of Medicine"

"When health is absent, wisdom cannot reveal itself, art cannot manifest, strength cannot fight, wealth becomes useless, and intelligence cannot be applied."

-Herophilus, Greek physician

"The first wealth is health."

-Ralph Waldo Emerson, American Essayist/Lecturer/
Philosopher

While you can't control much of what goes on around you, you can control what goes inside you. Most everything you consume is done by your choosing. Every piece of food you eat or tv you watch is your choice. Every drink you sip or piece of news you read is your choosing.

Sure, we're surrounded by advertisements in an ongoing bombardment of media propaganda that sneaks into our subconscious, but outside of this sliver of consumption, you remain in control of the other 95% of what you consume.

Although most of us can acknowledge that we do have control over what we consume, we struggle to change our habits of consumption. This is largely due to the dominant habit of consuming for short-term gratification rather than long-term health. We consume what our parents consume, what our friends consume, and what our society consumes. We consume what's convenient, comfortable, and affordable. We consume what we like, and we consume what we want.

Most Americans consume from the time they wake up until the time they go to bed. We eat breakfast, have a mid-morning snack, eat lunch, have a snack after work, eat dinner, and might have another snack before bed. We listen to the radio or a podcast on our way to and from work, we surf the internet while at work and watch Netflix before bed.

It feels like the only time we don't consume is when we're sleeping.

Which wouldn't be so heavy if our consumption was done consciously. Unfortunately, most of our consumption is not being done consciously. We are unconscious consumers.

So, let's break down our consumption through two primary lenses: food and media.

We'll start with food.

Our society continues to move through trends and fads in health and nutrition as we are continually developing a greater understanding of the human body. One year we eat egg whites, then only protein, then we go keto before jumping on the next bandwagon that rolls through town. These fads come and go as we are continually learning about health, nutrition, and the human body. The only constant here is change as our understanding of health is continually evolving.

A recent example of our evolving relationship with food is fat. We spent the last few decades hating on fat before we recently started to acknowledge how healthy some fats are. Healthy fats went from being grouped in with unhealthy fats and being perceived as one of the most unhealthy things for us to consume to becoming one of the healthiest.

While science attempts to provide explanations of life and the nature of existence, it's simply the best explanation they have from their current level of understanding. As they continue to level up, the scientific community gains deeper and further understanding of our bodies. Accepting science as fact is a slippery slope. They are doing the best they can with where they're at, but our understanding of the universe is limited. In general, most scientists aren't spiritual gurus.

Why do you think Einstein was able to create such impactful breakthroughs? My take is because he was so evolved spiritually. His work didn't come from an egoic place of mind, it came from a place of universal consciousness. Many scientists today are not in this place of being evolved spiritually.

So, how can you consume healthy foods that support you in living fully alive when you don't really know what's healthy?

In what often feels like a previous life, I spent a few years as a PE and Health teacher. Through these years, I learned some keys to a healthy diet.

I was teaching at an inner-city school where 100% of students received free lunch and breakfast, and the majority spoke English as a second language. Although most of these kids were out playing soccer every chance they got, they were still overweight. It didn't make sense until I started paying attention to their diet. They ate breakfast provided by the school, which consisted of prepackaged foods with an ingredient list 40 items long. Lunch was the same. For snacks, they ate Hot Cheetos. I didn't see kids eating fruits or vegetables.

It eventually occurred to me that fruits and vegetables are expensive. Hot Cheetos are cheap. On a Hot Cheeto diet, you can spend $1.50 and get 1000 calories. Unfortunately, these are not healthy calories. They start to add up. When you don't eat many natural foods for a few weeks straight, your health starts to suffer. The chemicals wear on you as your nutrients deplete.

Arguably, the most important aspect of our physical health is eating a balanced diet. In return, I eat copious amounts of fruits and vegetables. I make the majority of my food from natural ingredients, many of which are grown out in my garden.

Of all the changes and upgrades I've made to my lifestyle over the past 2 decades, changing to a plant-based diet has had one of the biggest effects. I have more energy and think more clearly. I look better and feel better. I don't get sick, am less emotional, and am more engaged in the world around me. I've found a diet that supports my body in being fully alive.

In general, food that comes from bags has preservatives and other ingredients that make them "taste good" and last long. The longer the list of ingredients, the less healthy the food. The shorter the ingredient list, the healthier the food. There are, of course, exceptions to this rule, but in general, it's good practice to stick with foods that have few ingredients.

Buy the peanut butter with one ingredient instead of the one with five.

Peanut butter needs one ingredient, ground peanuts (or two ingredients if you want salt).

Eat plants and vegetables. Broccoli has one ingredient. Broccoli. It's healthy, natural, high in protein, and delicious.

Eating fruits and vegetables can help reduce the risk of heart disease, type II diabetes, high blood pressure, and certain forms of cancer. They also have phytochemicals that "fight" to protect your health. They're low in calories and high in fiber, which helps control your weight. Not to mention the vitamins and nutrients they have.

While our bodies are each individualized with their own personal needs and preferences, one common theme amongst all body types is that plants are good for us.

Food is our energy source. Our energy -and all of the systems that run on our energy- is affected by the food we eat. When we consume natural, high vibrational foods, we can optimize the effectiveness of our systems. When we eat processed, lower vibrational foods, it clogs up our hardware. It slows our processing speed and limits our bandwidth. We can still do most of the things we want and need to do; it just takes longer and isn't as effective.

We don't necessarily need to eat natural foods. Most people can survive for 75 years eating whatever they want. But this book isn't about surviving; it's about thriving. It's hard to thrive when we feed ourselves fuel sources that lower our vibe. However, when we consume natural fuels that honor and support both our higher self and our operating systems, we can operate in more aligned and effective ways. New levels of hardware are unlocked, new abilities are discovered, and greater bliss is achieved.

One of my mentors came back from a nature conference in Colorado with a tool he connects to the leaves of plants called the PlantWave. The sensors on the PlantWave pick up the vibration of the plant, and turn these vibrations into sound. You can connect the device to a plant and literally listen to the plant's music. If you mist the plant with water, it generally sounds excited and happy. The same change in its music occurs if you gently touch it with love and kindness. Similarly, you can hear the difference in its sound if you are rough, violent, or rip off a leaf. This device brings the plant to life! It makes it almost impossible to deny that plants are living as it gives you the ability to listen to the plant react and respond to its environment. This tool shows that plants have consciousness.

Plants are alive with energy, consciousness, and DNA. When we consume them, their energy, consciousness, and DNA are absorbed into our body. When we eat synthesized, machine-made foods, these processed foods, and all their additives are absorbed into our bodies.

What do you think is better for you and your systems, the energy of machine-made meals or natural plants?

Natural foods help to center and ground us in our bodies while processed foods do the opposite as they disconnect or separate us from our body. We have more energy when eating natural foods and can more effectively regulate our emotions. Our diet directly affects our mental, emotional, and physical wellbeing. The better we eat, the better we feel.

We are also beginning to see the science of energy explain that everything has an energetic vibration. Plants have energy, and meat has energy. The problem is that most meat comes from factories where the animals are packed into a minimum amount of space, where they live in horrible conditions before they are brutally murdered in front of their family and friends. The negative energy of their life experience is stored in their body. When we eat their meat, we consume their low vibrational energy.

If, however, you go hunting and swiftly kill an animal who's living freely in nature, this animal will have a very different energy than one that was raised in the enslavement of our meat industry being pumped with hormones and steroids. Meat itself is not the problem. Humans have depended upon meat as a staple of our diet for thousands of years. The problem is that most of the meat we now consume is enslaved, tortured, and abused. This is not the kind of energy you want to put into your body.

More so, most meat has growth hormones, steroids, or other supplements added to help the animal grow big and fat. The bigger and fatter it is, the more food it creates. The more food it creates, the more money they make. Unfortunately, when you consume this meat, you consume the hormones, steroids, or supplements that have been added to it. These additives have an effect on you and your health. I was shocked by the difference I saw in my emotions when switching to a plant-based diet. The ups and downs I used to experience were replaced with a consistent stream of pleasant-ness. Sure, life still happens, and I still experience the full range of human emotion. The difference is that when I now experience an emotional shift to any state lesser than pleasant peace, I am able to locate the cause of the emotion and trace it back to an event, thought, belief, or occurrence that can be identified and integrated.

When I lived on meat, there were so many emotional waves that I didn't know what was what. It was hard to tie emotions to experiences or beliefs as there were so many different emotions going on. Granted, some of the ability to identify emotions and their roots is a result of the personal work I've done, but much of it is a result of removing the baggage of outside hormones and chemicals from my diet.

We operate more optimally when we consume high vibrational energy that is uplifting. This energy can be found abundantly in fruits and vegetables but is almost non-existent in packages of processed food. As we clean up our diet, we become more in touch with ourselves. We feel the effects different foods have on our systems and grow connected with our physical health. We begin to see the ties between our physical health and our mental, emotional, and spiritual health. We see the tie between our consumption and our emotions, our food and our energy levels. Eventually, we move to a place of acknowledging that our food is our energy. When we eat clean, we have clean, healthy energy, supporting our systems to operate smoothly. When we eat poorly, we have discordant, scrambled energy, and our systems struggle.

At the same time, if there's food you love that isn't the healthiest, you don't need to entirely deprive yourself. Find a healthy balance. When people go on intense diets that cut out all their pleasure foods, the diet is generally unsustainable. The goal here is creating a balanced diet based on healthy plants that's sustainable. We're not trying to eat healthy for a few weeks, we're trying to eat healthy for a lifetime.

One of the most concrete steps you can take to live more fully alive is cleaning up your diet. Studies have shown that a plant-based diet can help you live longer, will minimize your risk of stroke, improve your cholesterol, decrease the risk of cancer, help you lose weight, will help prevent type II diabetes, lower your blood pressure, and help keep your heart healthy. As your diet improves, you'll begin to experience upgrades to your systems. As these upgrades occur, your appreciation and gratitude for a plant-based diet will continue to deepen.

The other aspect of our diet that's worth examining is how often we eat.

As we continually develop new understandings of how our body most optimally functions, we find new information that can be applied to help our body operate more smoothly.

One of our newer understandings in regard to health is that our body needs breaks from eating. When we look back at our ancestors, we acknowledge they often went for long periods of time without eating. Not eating was natural for us as humans. In return, the research on Intermittent Fasting is phenomenal. I'll break down the basics.

The average American sleeps for 8 hours a day and is awake for 16 hours. Let's say we're awake from 7:00am-11:00pm. We generally eat breakfast around 8:00am then eat our last food for the day around 8:00pm. This is a schedule where you eat for 12 hours and fast for 12 hours. This is the average American eating schedule, a schedule that we are finding to be less than ideal.

With intermittent fasting, you eat for 8 hours and fast for 16 (10 hours of eating with 14 hours of fasting is better than 12 and 12 but not as good as 8 and 16 or 6 and 18). One popular Intermittent schedule is to push breakfast back until around 10 am, then eat your last food for the day around 6 pm. The times can be modified in a way that works for you, but the key is getting to the 16 hours of fasting. When doing so, your body enters a state of ketosis where it burns fat at a faster rate than normal. There are a variety of other benefits from intermittent fasting including lowering your risk for type 2 diabetes, reducing inflammation, improving heart health, preventing cancer, improving brain function, and preventing Alzheimer's.

There are other types of fasting that may have even greater health benefits. Of the different forms of fasting, dry fasting may be the most powerful. On a dry fast, you eat and drink nothing. No food. No liquid. Not even water. In the "Phoenix Protocol" by August Dunning (a former NASA Space Station scientist) he explains how dry fasting produces massive amounts of stem cells that can repair your body. Dry fasting reduces inflammation and restores your cells. I recently completed a 3 day dry fast and was amazed at how much energy I had, how clear my head felt, and how connected I became to my body. He claims that completing a seven day dry fast per year can reverse aging.

Equally important is that fasting brings awareness to your eating habits. When you practice fasting, eating becomes more of a conscious act, as increased awareness is placed around your consumption of food. You become aware of how often you eat out of habit or boredom rather than hunger. Through fasting, I found that I often eat for enjoyment. Fasting can teach you to eat when you are hungry, as opposed to simply eating out of habit.

Furthermore, fasting can serve as a powerful tool in redefining your relationship with hunger. Many people around the world expect to be full. Others are never full. We generally experience discomfort and unease when our body feels hungry. However, the more we sit with the experience of hunger, the more comfortable it becomes. Often, after emerging through the initial wave of perceived hunger, the body settles into a state of heightened awareness and clarity of thought that is hard to experience on a full stomach. Fasting gets easier with practice. That said, fasting is not easy. It's a mental, physical, and emotional challenge. It puts you outside of your comfort zone, deep into your growth zone. It's here that great evolution can occur.

Dr. Umar Faruq said, "Hunger is the first element of self-discipline. If you can control what you eat and drink, you can control everything else." Learning to be at peace with hunger is a major step in taking control of your thoughts, emotions, and health.

Fasting has also been used spiritually for thousands of years to help people connect more deeply with both their true self and the ultimate greater self. Again, fasting can help move us to a conscious place of increased awareness. The Native Americans used vision fasts as a right of passage where adolescents would go into the woods alone for a few days with nothing but some water and a pouch of tobacco to give the spirits when they came. They would come back with a new sense of self.

In Bill Plotkin's work with helping people find their eco niche, he often uses the vision fast as part of this process. He helps everyone prepare beforehand by setting intentions and getting in the right mental space before sending them into the woods for a few days alone with nothing. When they return from the vision fast, many of these individuals have found their life purpose. They have a renewed motivation and sense of self.

Again, humans spent thousands of years hungry. Hunger is a more natural state to exist in than that of being full. The last two hundred years have seen a dramatic shift in our relationship with food and hunger. Yet, our body evolves slower than society does. It takes the body a while to catch up. There may come a day when we operate as optimally on a full stomach as we do an empty one, but we are not there yet. Learn to embrace the hunger.

This leads to the final aspect of diet I'd like to touch on, the amount of food we consume. A healthy diet isn't just about what we consume and when we consume it. It also includes how much we consume. Granted, the quantity isn't nearly as significant as the quality, as we can eat as much broccoli and carrots as we want without seeing adverse health effects. But quantity does matter. When we oversaturate ourselves with more fuel than we need, it takes effort for our body to process the food and return to a balanced state of harmony.

We've probably all experienced the drag of overeating. We know the lethargy overeating can invoke and have sat with the discomfort of being stuffed. It's not a good feeling.

When overeating is regularly experienced over the course of years, our body suffers. Our systems slow down as motivation decreases and discomfort increases. Health issues arise. We don't look as good, and we don't feel as good. We suffer.

When we observe the spectrum from gluttony to starvation, we see that when we have the option, much of humanity errors more on the side of gluttony than we do starvation. A healthy relationship with food allows us to exist in a balanced place between the two, where we eat when we need to eat and refrain from food when we're good.

There are some tangible tricks you can apply to help regulate your food intake:

- Drink a glass of water before you eat. It fills your belly, making it feel more full as you eat.

- Put an appropriate amount of food on your plate, and don't go back for seconds.

- Brush your teeth when you get hungry.

- Eat slow. It takes your brain 20-30 minutes to tell your body it's full.

Yes, food is incredible. It's one of the greatest pleasures of Earthly form. It provides us with energy and enjoyment. It's uplifting, grounding, and fun. Food is magical when we consciously consume a healthy quantity of quality food. However, food can also cause health struggles, energetic deficiencies, and emotional turmoil. Food can serve us or hinder us. It can raise our vibration or lower it. Food can empower us to live fully alive, or it can disempower us into a state of discordant lethargy.

By placing awareness on what we consume, and when we consume it, we can use food as a tool to align our physical body with our highest self in a way that supports us in living more fully alive.

The food we consume and how often we consume it plays a major role in not only our health but our overall state of being.

While on the topic of consumption, there's another primary aspect of consumption we should touch on. The two things we consume the most are food and media. Let's observe our consumption of media.

Media is everything we watch, read, and listen to. There's an energetic vibration attached to every piece of media you consume. Media has the ability to uplift and inspire you or detach and reject you.

When you listen to negative stories of all the "bad" things happening in the world, your body takes on the energy of all these "bad" things.

Have you ever watched a scary movie then found yourself feeling scared? Your body took on the energy of the movie. The movie affected the way you felt.

When you consume low vibrational content, your vibration lowers. As your vibration lowers, so does your health.

At the same time, when you consume high vibrational content that is uplifting and inspiring, it raises your vibration.

There are currently a variety of scientists, astrophysicists, and spiritual seekers developing new understandings of our reality. Consuming these new perspectives and insights of conscious information can help raise your vibration. These forms of media can shift your perspective in a way that serves you. They can help to expand your awareness and deepen your intelligence in a way that improves your quality of life and supports you in living more fully alive. Try listening to the Aubrey Marcus Podcast. Check out Dr. Joe Dispenza, Bruce Lipton, Michio Kaku, and Neil Degrass Tyson. Listen to Alan Watts. Watch David Attenborough's films.

This book is a piece of conscious media that will hopefully do the same.

As is most of the conscious content being created today.

Unfortunately, not all content is of a high vibration. The reality is that much of the content in today's world is of a lower vibration as it's created with the goal of generating as much money as possible, rather than supporting humanity as much as possible. Most of humanity would rather zone out looking at pretty people in a silly movie than consume something that informs.

The point here is that much like the food we consume, the media we consume affects our overall health and wellbeing. We can consume inspiring, uplifting media that aligns and inspires us, or we can consume negative and upsetting media that causes discord and discomfort.

This media we consume will either support us in feeling inspired and uplifted or detached and discordant.

The media we consume not only affects our health but our overall state of being.

Think about the way you feel when listening to intense rock music as opposed to the way you feel when listening to the calming sounds of nature. Think about how the nightly news makes you feel. Now think about how you feel when reading an uplifting book. How do you feel after watching a great comedy? What about a scary movie?

When we sit with the feelings we experience in each of these different forms of media consumption, it becomes hard to deny that what we consume affects our being. When we consume uplifting, inspiring content, we are uplifted and inspired. When we consume scary or upsetting content, we feel scared or upset.

This fact was clearly demonstrated by Dr. Emoto in his famous Water Crystal Experiment. He took a freezing metal plate and played a variety of different songs and words into the plate. He then let a water droplet fall onto the plate, instantly freezing itself into crystal form. The crystals that formed when words of love and light were played into the plate were crystals of balance, harmony, and utter beauty. The crystals that formed when words of negativity or anger were played were scattered, jagged, and unappealing. After going through dozens of different words and songs, Dr. Emoto reminds us that our body is 70% water. More importantly, so is our planet.

In observing Dr. Emoto's water crystals, it becomes undeniable that our consumption affects the way we feel. He made it visible.

After seeing his work, I started sharing it with my students. It always resonated with them as, year after year, the students would start referring to the way their water felt after watching his work. Water makes up 70% of your body. When your water is aligned in balance and harmony, receiving positive input and inspiration, your body feels aligned in harmony. You feel aware and inspired. You shift toward being fully alive.

When you gain awareness of what you consume and how that consumption affects the way you feel, you can make the changes necessary to support your body in feeling the way you want to feel as opposed to continuing feeling the ways you've always felt.

Yet, despite the significance of everything outlined above, the most important aspect of your physical health may be lifestyle. Your lifestyle is the way you live your life. What do you do on a day-to-day basis? Are you standing or sitting? How much do you walk and move your body? Are you active? What do you do for fun? Does your lifestyle consist of healthy habits?

Many of today's health-conscious individuals haven't been to the gym in years but are now in the best shape of their life. They no longer play sports, they don't go to fitness classes, and they don't have personal trainers. Rather, they simply use their body. They create a healthy lifestyle. They go for walks daily. They play with their children. They develop a daily yoga routine and mix in some exercises for their core.

An exercise routine does not need to be anything crazy. 30 minutes of exercise a few times a week is great. Once a week, go on a longer hike. Mix some physical activities into your daily lifestyle. Do what your body needs to feel healthy and alive. Take care of it. Listen to it. Learn to partner your diet with your lifestyle in a way that works for you. This is key. Find what works for you. Pay attention to the way you feel. Listen to your joints and muscles. Listen to your stomach and heart. Become connected to your body. Stop doing things your body doesn't like. Do more of what it does.

Stop eating food that doesn't make you feel good. Eat more food that lifts you up. Find a form of exercise that you enjoy. Use your body. Work with your hands. Build things. Dig in the earth. Play with kids. Walk on our planet.

There are so many forms of physical activity and exercise. It doesn't matter what form of exercise you use as long as you exercise. Find a form of exercise that works for you. And exercise. We need to move our bodies.

If we look back on our ancestors, we see they spent thousands of years nomadically, on the move, hunting and gathering their food, continually using their bodies. Using the body is in our DNA. It's part of being human.

The more we use the body, the better shape it stays in. When we get lazy, our physical health suffers. If we stay lazy for too long, we generally develop injury and disease. The better health we're in, the more we can do with our bodies. If we grow out of shape or become unhealthy, our options as to what we can do with our body decrease.

Above, I touched on the importance of listening to the body.

Unfortunately, this is a struggle for many. When we experience general discomfort on a regular basis, it's hard to acknowledge that we are experiencing discomfort. Our body learns to normalize the discomfort. If we carry around 40 pounds of extra weight for a few years, this heaviness becomes our new norm. In this norm, we become accustomed to being tired and having low energy.

When we're unhealthy, it becomes difficult to remember what it feels like to be healthy. We think we're ok. We think we feel fine. Our body is an incredibly powerful manipulator. It deceives us. It normalizes our unhealthiness. This makes it difficult to make the changes necessary to return to a place of physical health.

That is to say, our bodies' ability to acclimate to physical discomfort makes it difficult for us to acknowledge where we're off and get ourselves back to a physically healthy place.

We typically enable our unhealthy lifestyle until things get bad. More often than not, we eventually experience a wake-up call. A heart attack. A bout of cancer. Pneumonia. Type 2 diabetes. Whatever it is, it shakes our foundation. It reminds us that we're not healthy. It might even tell us that we haven't been healthy for a long time.

Fortunately, it's never too late to take control of your health.

Now, there may be residual effects from the years of abuse you put your body through, but you can still turn yourself into a shrine of health.

This said, changing old habits can be difficult.

The oral gratification of chips and sugar is hard to overcome.

But overcoming this gratification is so worth it.

No dessert can compare to the high you get when becoming the master of your domain. When you rise to take control over your health, you consciously choose everything you consume. You choose what you consume. This not only transforms your health but improves multiple aspects of your life, as health is a foundational aspect of your overall well-being.

When you're healthy in your physical body, you not only have more energy, greater mental clarity, and increased control over your emotions, you're also more aligned with your highest self. When you hold honor and respect for your physical body, it will not only remember how to optimize itself here in the physical realm, but it will let you know what changes or modifications need to be made. The more you listen to your body, the healthier you become. The healthier you become, the more smoothly your systems operate.

You're more fully alive when you're healthy.

You look better and feel better. You think better and are better.

When you're healthy, you can thrive in a state of being fully alive.

Chapter 10 Summary

Recap:

- We are primarily unconscious consumers. Consume consciously.
- Natural foods (fruits and vegetables) are the healthiest foods. The fewer ingredients, the better.
- Food is energy. Eat food that's aligned with the energetic state you want to experience.
- Get comfortable with hunger.
- Consciously consume media that serves you. Refrain from media that does not.
- Observe your lifestyle. The more you use your body, the healthier it will be.
- Listen to your body. It's brilliant.

Questions to consider:

- What modifications can you make to consume more consciously?
- How can you improve your diet?
- How are your energy levels? When in the day do you have the best energy? When is your energy lacking? What can you do to improve your energy levels?
- How is the media you consume serving you? How is it harming you?
- When you check-in and listen to your body, what does it tell you?

Challenge:

- Complete a 5 day cleanse or a 3 day fast. It doesn't so much matter what cleanse or fast you do. It's the dedication and commitment that matters. In committing to following the guidelines of the cleanse/fast, you will become more conscious of your consuming habits. You'll notice when you eat habitually, when you consume emotionally, and when you consume out of boredom. Through the process, practice bringing awareness to your consumption. After completing the cleanse/fast, reflect upon your habits around consumption. How can you move forward consuming more consciously?

Next Level Challenge:

- Complete a 3 day Dry Fast. This means that you eat and drink nothing. Not only will you get all the benefits listed above, your body will also repair its cells, create stem cells, and implement a variety of other health benefits. You can read about the dry fast in "The Phoenix Protocol" by August Dunning.

CHAPTER 11

Being in your Mind

Your mind creates your reality.
Create it consciously.

"Reality exists in the human mind, and nowhere else."
-George Orwell, English novelist, journalist, and critic.

"All problems are illusions of the mind."
-Eckhart Tolle, German born spiritual teacher and self-help author.

"If you realized how powerful your thoughts are, you would never think a negative thought."
-Peace Pilgrim, American spiritual teacher, mystic, and activist.

"With our thoughts, we make the world."
-Buddha, Ancient Indian religious leader, ascetic, and teacher.

"None but ourselves can free our minds."
-Bob Marley, Jamaican singer, songwriter, and musician.

To live fully alive, you must learn to control your thoughts. For, they combine with your beliefs to create your reality. Your reality is a result of your thoughts and your beliefs.

We'll examine both these aspects of reality.

Let's begin with thoughts.

In a 2020 study on 184 people by a team of researchers in Canada, they found that we have an average of 6,200 thoughts per day.

How many of these thoughts are you aware of? At the same time, how many of these thoughts are just running in the background of your operating system, subconsciously, outside of your awareness?

More so, how many of these thoughts are positive and serve you? How many are negative and hold you back?

Your thoughts control much of your day-to-day experience. The thoughts and memories you have around the occurrences of your life largely affect the way you feel about them. A concrete example is the old question of whether the cup is half full or half empty. What do you think about the cup and the water? Do you see the cup as having water, a beautiful and foundational aspect of existence that fills you with gratitude and appreciation? Or do you see it as not being enough, a cup that is only partly full, not fulfilling your expectations or desires?

It's the same cup with the same water. The only thing that changes is the thought- the perception- of the cup and water.

This analogy can be used to observe all your thoughts.

Do you see people as being complete and full, beautiful exactly as they are?

Or do you see people as lacking and incomplete, needing to do, or be, more?

Do you see yourself as beautiful and whole, continually learning and growing, complete exactly as you are?

Or do you see yourself as lesser than and lacking, focusing on your flaws and all that is not good enough?

This concept can be applied to every aspect of your life: your job, family, relationships, health, finances, and the list goes on.

Are you feeling grateful for the benefits of your job or frustrated with the flaws?

Do you have all the money you need to live fully, or do you need more?

Do you love and appreciate your family for who they are, or do you wish they would change?

What you think about the people and occurrences around you directly affects your day-to-day living. You are closer to living fully alive when you think positive thoughts that inspire you and uplift you. When you think negative thoughts about other people, your environment, work, or any other aspect of life, the negative thoughts will deflate you and cause you to feel crappy.

What you think about your life and the world you exist in directly affects your relationship with yourself and the world around you.

The better you think, the better you live.

The problem is that most of us are only aware of a fraction of the thoughts we have each day. If we're not aware of what we're thinking, we can allow negative thoughts to come in. These negative thoughts can turn into negative stories and in turn, create negative behavior.

While you might not have the bandwidth to gain awareness around each of the thoughts you have on any given day, you can take time to sit still with yourself and acknowledge what you truly think and feel about the different aspects of your life. Through the process of sitting in silent stillness, you can find the roots of your thoughts and beliefs. Although you might not catch every individual thought you have on food or religion, you can develop an understanding of your core belief on food and religion. From this core belief, your individual thoughts will grow.

I was always frugal. I rarely spent money on things that weren't necessary and would always hunt for the best deal when I did need to buy something. Whenever there was the option to do something myself rather than pay someone else to do it, I did it. I was never in debt (besides those tens of thousands of dollars of college debt we all carried), but I never had much extra either.

When I started doing deep work on myself, I suddenly became aware of the negative beliefs I carried toward money. I thought money was for greedy people who didn't care about humanity. I thought it was a product of a flawed system used to regulate and control us. Money was the root of all evil.

These beliefs came from a childhood in which I grew up poor. My parents were always stressed about money as we had some tough times financially. I also had a dad who despised the Federal Reserve and fought to restore the gold and silver standard.

In return, I developed negative thoughts about money. These negative thoughts evolved into negative stories that led me to create an unhealthy relationship with money.

Once I developed awareness around the thoughts and beliefs I held toward money, I was able to start shifting them. But as long as they existed in a blind spot, they continued to infiltrate my life in negative ways.

I've now evolved my beliefs on money to positive ones. I see money as an exchange of value. When we provide value, we're compensated with money. It gives us the opportunity to do good in the world and live freely. It makes life easier and more fun.

As my beliefs on money have changed, my thoughts and actions have followed. I now live in abundance.

There's an old concept of, "Fake it till you make it". This idea is based on the belief that if you tell yourself you can do it, that you have the skills, abilities, focus, and dedication to make it happen, then you will make it happen. If you think that you can do it then you can do it. But if you think that you are not ready, or not good enough, then you are not ready, and you are not good enough.

Early in President Obama's presidency, he was asked about how prepared he was to be President of the United States of America. He responded by explaining that no one can ever be ready to be president. There's no preparation you can have to prepare you for that job. He explained that he was as prepared as he could be. The best he could do now was surround himself with smart people, show up every day, and do the best he could.

Political beliefs aside, If he thought he wasn't ready to be president, he wouldn't have been ready to be president. If he thought he was ready, then he was ready.

Similarly, my spiritual teacher was once encouraging me to start holding space for others. I replied explaining that I was still embodying the concepts and did not yet master many of them. She responded by stating, "If everyone waited until they were masters to teach, we would have no teachers."

I was ready to start teaching when I thought I was ready.

This said, your mind is smart. It's pulling information from the experiences you've had, the books you've read, conversations had, and every other aspect of your existence. It knows what you've done and what you haven't. It also knows where you excel and where you struggle. It knows you as well as anyone.

If nurtured, your mind can become one of your greatest allies. If not, it can be an army of resilience. Through meditation, you can nurture this relationship and develop a positive relationship with your mind so it can support you in fully thriving. Through meditation, you gain awareness around your thoughts. From here, you can shift the negative thoughts that interfere and nurture the positive thoughts that support you. Your mind will become kinder. You and your mind will understand each other better and see each other in a new light. A bond will form between your thoughts and your awareness. In this bond, you can consciously choose what you think. You can't lie to yourself because you know. You take control of the thoughts you are forming and consciously shift them when they do not serve you.

If you haven't put in the work to start your business, you're not going to convince yourself that you have. But if you have done the work and are just caught up on fear or self-doubt, you can consciously choose to change these thoughts. Any self-limiting thought you think can be consciously changed.

It starts with developing that relationship with the mind. Meditation is one of the most powerful modalities to develop this relationship. Meditate. Daily. Sit with yourself, and take control of your thoughts.

Your thoughts hold energy that has the power to create.

This power of thought is not limited. The power extends to each and every thought you think.

If you think positively about someone, your body creates positive emotions and affiliations with that person. If you think negatively about them, your body creates negative emotions and affiliations with them.

If you think something is wrong or bad, then it will continue to be wrong or bad for as long as you think of it in those terms.

But, if you can remove your judgment and move past the thoughts of right or wrong, good or bad, you can see things as they are. You see that they are just doing what they're meant to be doing, being what they're being. They just are. They are not good or bad; they are.

Good and bad are thought perceptions that *we* place upon things.

When we remove labels, things are free to simply be.

As you improve your ability to control your thoughts, you can learn to catch yourself when you place judgment upon things. Eventually, you become aware of negative thoughts or beliefs as they enter your mind, and you do not allow yourself to hold onto them. You stop holding space for thoughts that do not serve you. You can then replace these thoughts with positive, uplifting ones that align with your highest self and support you in living fully alive.

Again, the best practice I've found for gaining awareness and control over thoughts is meditation. Through meditation, we actively train ourselves to control our thoughts. There are a variety of meditation techniques, all of which share the common thread of controlling thought. Meditation teaches us to take control of the mind rather than allowing the mind to control us. Meditation is a conscious practice in presence and awareness. By sitting in a quiet and calm space, and placing awareness on our breathing, we gain a greater connection with our true essence. In this place, we can connect with our highest self while gaining insights and understandings of our current self.

In "The Yoga Of The Bhagavad Gita", Paramahansa Yogananda states, "Through each triumphant contact with spirit, in meditation, the soul consciousness becomes strengthened and more firmly in control of the bodily kingdom. Even the novitiate meditator quickly finds that he is able to draw upon the spiritual power and consciousness of the inner world of soul and spirit to enlighten his bodily kingdom and activities-physical, mental, and spiritual."

Meditation leads to connection and control of the bodily kingdom.

As we develop a greater connection with ourselves, we gain control over our thoughts and can see how powerful they truly are. We see how we struggle when we allow negative thoughts in, and we see how we thrive when we focus our thoughts on gratitude, awe, love, and light. So much of your day-to-day experience is based on what you think of it. If you think high vibrational thoughts, you have a high vibrational experience. High vibrational experiences lift and inspire you. They are the kind of experiences we all want to have. And they are the types of experiences you can have when you learn to control your thoughts.

The more you practice the skill of controlling your thoughts, the better you get at it. The better you get, the more control you gain over them. The more control you have of your thoughts, the more you can align them to support you in living fully alive.

This leads to your beliefs. Beliefs are thoughts that you accept as truth.

One way to develop a belief is by researching a topic and weighing a variety of information before creating a belief of your own. This is a proactive, conscious approach to the formation of beliefs. Unfortunately, very few people form their beliefs with this calculated approach. Most people form most of their beliefs by accepting what others say as truth. This is how beliefs are generally formed in children. Parents explain things a certain way, and the child believes things to be that way. These beliefs will remain until they are consciously observed and changed. If you never go back to re-examine the beliefs you developed through your parents' lens, you generally find yourself believing much of what you did as a child. This is why so many people follow the same religion as their parents, eat a similar diet, vote for the same political party, and have the same traditions. It's only when you consciously question the belief that you can change your religion, stop voting for the Republicrat, clean up your diet, and create your own traditions.

If you never question or challenge the beliefs that were installed in you as a child, they won't really change. Asking yourself, "what do I believe because my parents believed?" can be an incredibly powerful practice. Try creating a list of all the beliefs you hold that your parents held. Then, question them. Which of these beliefs serve you and support you in fully thriving? From here, you can continue to support the beliefs that are in your best interest and shift the ones that are not.

When you have awareness around your beliefs, you can work with them. They can evolve and grow. The issue is that most people are unaware of so many of their beliefs. Many beliefs are acquired subconsciously during childhood. What you believe when you're 10 is what you believe when you're 40 if you don't consciously examine the belief and update it.

This holds true for what you believe about yourself, your family and friends, money, religion, and the world you exist in.

What do you believe to be true about yourself? What do you believe to be true of the world you live in? What about the media? Government? Religion?

The beliefs you hold shape the world you exist in, as your beliefs create much of your perceived reality.

If you believe the media has your best interest in mind and tells the truth, then you probably listen to the media and believe what they say. At the same time, if you believe the media to be a bi-product of a broken system based on financial gains and suppression of the people, you don't take much merit in what they say, or if you do, you take it with a grain of salt.

When you believe you're healthy, you are healthy. When you believe you are wealthy, you are wealthy. When you believe you are an incredible, powerful, beautiful human being, you are an incredible, powerful, beautiful human being.

The catch here is that your mind is really smart. The "fake it till you make it" approach can be helpful in the short term, but eventually, your mind is going to catch on. It will become apparent that you don't really believe yourself. You might not believe you are ready for the job. You might not believe you are good enough.

In order to foundationally change your beliefs on either yourself or the world around you, you need to work your way back to the roots of your beliefs. Where do your beliefs originate? Why do you believe yourself to be the person you believe yourself to be? Why do you believe the world to be the way you believe it to be?

Again, your thoughts and beliefs are generally developed during childhood. You then integrate these thoughts and beliefs of yourself and your society into the life you create. These beliefs are primarily acquired subconsciously, without a conscious decision of whether or not they are beliefs you actually believe. You acquire your beliefs in childhood, then watch them play out through adulthood, with most people never re-examining them, allowing them to update and grow as you and your life evolves. If you never go back to re-examine your beliefs, you can find yourself at 80 years old, still seeing the world as you did as an 18-year-old.

Without the re-evaluation phase, you continue to accept the world in the same way you always have. If you don't critically observe the lens through which you view the world, you will see it through the same lens your whole life.

Fortunately, your brain is an incredibly intelligent and complex organ that can reprogram itself throughout its lifetime. Through recent findings in neuroplasticity, we are developing a better understanding of how our brain works.

Psychology Today gives a great explanation of neuroplasticity. They state that:

> "Neuroplasticity is the brain's capacity to continue growing and evolving in response to life experiences. Plasticity is the capacity to be shaped, molded, or altered; neuroplasticity, then, is the ability for the brain to adapt or change over time, by creating new neurons and building new networks.
>
> Historically, scientists believed that the brain stopped growing after childhood. But current research shows that the brain is able to continue growing and changing throughout the lifespan, refining its architecture or shifting functions to different regions of the brain.
>
> The importance of neuroplasticity can't be overstated: It means that it is possible to change dysfunctional patterns of thinking and behaving and to develop new mindsets, new memories, new skills, and new abilities."

Below are two additional quotes on neuroplasticity that provide further insight and perspective.

> "Because of the power of neuroplasticity, you can, in fact, reframe your world and rewire your brain so that you are more objective. You have the power to see things as they are so that you can

respond thoughtfully, deliberately, and effectively to everything you experience."

-Elizabeth Thorton

"Meditation invokes that which is known in neuroscience as neuroplasticity; which is the loosening of the old nerve cells or hardwiring in the brain, to make space for the new to emerge."

-Craig Krishn

Neuroscience is empowering. It shows that you can continue evolving and growing your brain and beliefs throughout the extent of your lifetime. Your beliefs are not fixed. Your skills don't stop developing. New neural pathways will continue being made as long as you continue to experience life. Your brain wants to grow and evolve. You just need to show up with an open mindset.

With this information, you can examine your beliefs, question them, and hold space for them to evolve. As you obtain new information and gain new experiences, your beliefs can evolve. You just need to make the space for this process to unfold naturally. You need to get out of your own way and allow your brain to do its thing. Stop holding to the past. Accept that just because you believed something to be a certain way at one point in your life, it doesn't mean it's still the same way or will remain that way indefinitely.

The universal law of impermanence states the only constant is change. Everything around you is constantly changing. And, your mind wants to do the same. You just need to let go of what you believe to be true and allow your beliefs to evolve with the world around you.

The last aspect of thoughts and beliefs I'd like to touch on involves the spectrum of truth. This is related to the law of equal and opposites. Polarity.

We live in a world of duality. For every up, there's a down. For black, there's white.

In return, we tend to see the world through these terms.

Right and wrong. Good and bad. Alive and dead.

It is, or it's not.

Generally, if the current scientific community accepts something as truth, we believe it to be true. If they don't, we don't. When we partner our trust in science with mainstream media consumption, we are fed a stream of truths and non-truths.

But what if we saw it differently?

Instead of it being yes or no, I believe, or I don't, what if it was "maybe, and"? Maybe that's true, as I can see their perspective, and, at the same time, I think this is also true. This is an inclusive mindset that holds space for all truths.

Or, what if all truths existed on a spectrum of truth instead of being a hard yes or no?

What if we were able to understand all sides of an argument and hold space for the possibility for any and all of them to be true?

Maybe this side is true, and maybe that side is true.

I started working to adapt this mindset a few years back and have found that often, there is truth to both sides. While one side may be perceived as more truthful than the other, generally, there are multiple truths. Instead of looking at it as one side or the other, maybe it could be 70-30. I believe one side to be 70% true and the other around 30% true.

Yeah, aliens probably exist; they're pretty high for me at around 97%.

But there's a chance there isn't anyone else out there and we are the only life in the universe. It looks like there's more evidence pointing to there being intelligent life than not, but holding space for both possibilities opens you to a more abundant mindset.

An abundant mindset begins opening you to new realms of possibility.

Instead of believing 100% that you live on after death, explore the possibility of not living on. How does it feel to think this is the only life you will ever live?

Conversely, if you are someone who believes that when you die, there is no more, life comes to a terminal end, and that's it, try to explore the possibility of life after death. How does this feel?

There is power in questioning your beliefs. Either you come out with a deeper understanding of your belief, or your belief shifts and upgrades. Both outcomes are beneficial.

If you can then hold space for both sides of the belief to be true, you are again in the mindset of abundance.

This perspective can be applied to most of your thoughts and beliefs.

Sure, Jeffrey Epstein's child sex ring was 100% wrong. There are some things that are hard to see another side to.

But most things do have another side.

There's a chance that our politicians do have our best interest in mind. There's a chance they actually care about our environment and the wellbeing of the middle class, and there's a chance that Covid really was as dangerous as they tried to make us believe. It's not a good chance. But there is a chance.

Yes, making lots of money gives us financial freedom. But it comes with a cost. Yes, breakups and separations are incredibly painful and difficult, AND they're often the best thing for us. Yes, there are truths in what the media reports and there are non-truths in what the media reports.

There are some things that are mostly true and others that are barely true.

Let's again use our politicians as an example. There is likely false information and exaggerations coming from their camps. But there's most likely some legitimacy to their stories. Few stories are fabricated from nothing. So with politicians, maybe it's like 50% nonsense and noise, 50% legitimacy.

From this perspective, we can hear the left on ABC and the right on FOX, the alternative media online, our social media feeds, whatever we read on Medium, and whoever's talking to Joe Rogan, and hold space for all of it. We can then find our own truth somewhere amongst all the other truths.

I find it hard to believe that any one source can be 100% true. Can any one perspective be 100% truthful? Few things are absolute truth.

If all possible truths existed on a continuum from 0% true to 100% true, few of them would be at the extreme ends. Most truths convene toward the middle.

70-30. 60-40.

70% chance ghosts and spirits are here amongst us. 30% they are not.

I've had two experiences where I'm pretty positive I saw ghosts. But was it my eyes and senses messing with me? I hold space for both possibilities.

I see a 65% chance we see the financial system collapse in our lifetime and a 35% chance we don't.

The part of me that thinks we will see the system collapse tries to be prepared, while the part of me that doesn't allows me to live in peace.

In allowing space for multiple truths, our perspectives and beliefs become more well-rounded, inclusive, open, and whole.

Opening ourselves to these possibilities also begins freeing us from the emotional attachment we have toward things being a certain way. If we see the Democrats as the problem, we view everything they do as bad. We get emotionally invested.

When we hold the possibility of both sides being equally corrupt or both sides being equally legit, we become less attached emotionally.

And again, most likely, there's some truth, and some noise, to all of it.

The separation from your last "failed" relationship wasn't their fault, and it wasn't your fault; it was both of you.

The pharmaceutical industry does some good, and it does some bad. They aren't pure evil. Sure, they're on the negative side of that 80-20 range, but they still do some good.

The same can be said for the oil and meat industries.

They are not good, and they are not bad. They are. They do what they do.

I don't agree with the way they're doing business, and I don't care for the lack of morality they display, but I understand why they enslave animals, pump them with hormones and steroids, and spray their plants with chemicals.

I don't support them. I eat plants and drive as minimally as possible, but I understand their perspective. They're making lots of money, providing jobs to millions, and contributing to the economy. They're just playing the game, participating in the systems that have been created. They're capitalists, capitalizing on the flawed systems in place.

As I've developed this mindset of seeing all sides, I've experienced a variety of concrete benefits along the way. One of my favorites is greater empathy for others. It feels like this comes from an increased ability to see their perspective. It's also helped me to detach from some unhealthy beliefs I held.

Additionally, I've noticed that in opening my perspective, I became aware of other sides of myself while developing a greater sense of peace and gratitude for things as they are.

I now find the mindset of "maybe and" to be far more beneficial than the "yes or no" mindset. It helped me navigate Covid as this mindset supports the perspective that we don't know for sure what's real and what is not. Make the best choices you can, with the information you have, while holding space for any and all of it to be true.

And, as information changes, know that it's often beneficial to change your mind. Your thoughts and beliefs can be outgrown.

Because all information exists somewhere on the spectrum of truth. We'll probably never know for sure where exactly the truth lies, so I hold the possibility for all of it to be true. In doing so, open yourself to the endless possibilities the universe beholds while knowing the only thing we know is that we don't know a thing.

Chapter 11 Summary

Recap:

- Your thoughts combine with your beliefs to create your reality.
- Your mind is smart. You might be able to fool it temporarily but not long term.
- Your thoughts are powerful. They carry energy. Choose them wisely.
- Meditation is a great tool to gain awareness around your thoughts.
- Beliefs are thoughts you are convinced to be true. They are arguably even more powerful than your thoughts.
- Neuroplasticity has taught us that the mind is continually growing and evolving.
- All truths exist on a spectrum of truth. Few truths are absolute.

Questions to consider:

- How much awareness do you have around your thoughts?
- Why do you believe that which you believe? Which of your beliefs might not be true?
- What thoughts or beliefs do you hold that do not serve you?

Challenge:

- Look within to find three truths you believe that do not serve you. These could be beliefs about yourself, others, or the world you live in. Find three limited beliefs you hold. Then, look for evidence that opposes your belief. Find evidence that can help rewire this belief. From here, rewrite these beliefs in a way that serves you. Continue looking for evidence to prove your new belief true. Transform the limited beliefs to become beliefs that empower and serve you.

Being in Habit

Humans are habitual beings.
Allow your habits to uplift and inspire you.

"We are what we repeatedly do. Excellence, then, is not an act, but a habit."

-Aristotle, Classical Greek philosopher and polymath

"Humans are imperfect creatures. You don't 'succeed' because you have no weaknesses; you succeed because you find your unique strengths and focus on developing habits around them."

-Tim Ferriss, American entrepreneur, author, podcast host, and lifestyle guru.

"If you believe you can change - if you make it a habit - the change becomes real."

-Charles Duhigg, American author and journalist.

Human beings are habitual beings. We create positive habits that are healthy and beneficial to our being, and we create negative habits that are unhealthy and detrimental to our being.

At the Media Lab of the Massachusetts Institute of Technology, they are putting custom-made electronic "black boxes" on students so researchers can monitor them going about their day. The devices record where the wearers go and how fast, their tone of voice, and subtle details about their body language. In doing so, they've found that about 90 percent of what most people do in any day follows routines. 90%!

We are habitual beings.

We routinely move about our day, doing things the same way as we did them yesterday, which just so happens to be the same way we did them the day before yesterday, and the day before that. We form habits that subconsciously rule our day-to-day existence. We have a habit of waking up slowly (or quickly) which is followed by a habit of going to the bathroom (or doing whatever you do next). This habit is followed by another habit that will be followed by yet another. The chain continues throughout most of the day until you go to bed, wake up, and repeat. We then do it all again tomorrow.

Fortunately, we still make choices within our habits. We have a habit of getting dressed at a certain time, maybe even in a certain way, but we generally choose our clothes. Some people consciously choose what food they eat or what they do for fun after work. While most people operate in a habitual fashion, they experience an element of free will within the confines of their habits.

Free will is good for us. Conscious decision making is even better. The more we consciously make decisions, the more alive and engaged we are in our existence. The more we passively live out of habit, the more we become a passenger in our own life.

One of the primary goals in the lens of "Being in Habit" is to gain awareness of your habits and consciously decide if these habits serve you. Are your daily habits supporting you in living the life you want to live? Do your habits uplift and inspire you or cause limitations and frustrations?

Developing consciousness around your habits helps move you toward a place of *being*.

This is not only powerful and empowering, but it is a step toward personal freedom. Every time you choose what you do, you are taking control of that moment in your life. Each step out of habit is a step away from sleep walk and into awareness.

When you sleepwalk through your life habits, you continue to exist in a zombified space of slumber.

When you consciously choose what you do, you awaken to an empowered place of creation. Last night, after I finished my work for the day, my brain felt tired, and I thought about just scrolling around on the internet. Instead, I consciously decided to play music. There was something inside calling me to play. So, I made the decision to put down the computer and pick up the guitar. A beautiful song unfolded. It was powerful and profound. I was in the conscious place of creation rather than an unconscious place of scrolling.

This is a major transformation that can permeate positive effects into all aspects of life.

In this space of being aware of your habits and actively choosing what you do, you learn to consciously choose how you respond to the world around you. In this space, you gain the ability to make healthy choices in regards to consumption, friends, emotions, and hobbies.

In this space, we become the creators of our existence.

This is a place of *being*. In this place, you make conscious decisions that align with your true self. In this place, you develop awareness around all aspects of your day and actively engage in living it.

A concrete way you can begin developing this awareness is by creating a list of all your habits. Track everything you do for a standard 24 to 48 hours. Do it on an average Tuesday. Record each step of your day.

Then, go through the list and mark each step that was habitual. This will bring attention to the habits.

Next, declare if each of those habits are "positive" or "negative". Is this habit serving you or suppressing you? Is it inspiring you or distracting you? Does it provide freedom or restraint? Give each of the habits you listed a ranking of 1-5, with 1 being a "negative" habit and 5 being a "positive" habit.

After creating this list, reflect upon it. What effects do these habits have on your overall quality of life? What effects do these habits have on your relationships, your health, and your happiness?

Then, after creating a list of your habits, and reflecting on their effects, decide which of these habits could be removed and replaced with either a positive habit, or unstructured time.

Unstructured time is free time for you to choose what you want to do. This is different from the time you set aside to watch Netflix. This is free time where you consciously decide what you want to do. You can encourage yourself to do something different with this time every day. Where in your schedule can you create an hour of free time for you to consciously choose what you want to do?

The practice of scheduling time for you to consciously choose what you do can be a powerful tool in developing awareness around what you're doing. By taking time to choose what to do, you begin gaining awareness around all the times you are subconsciously acting in habit.

You eventually begin to feel the energetic difference between **doing** out of conscious choosing vs. **doing** habitually. You'll like the feeling of consciously choosing and do more of it.

When we're consciously choosing what we're doing, we're moving toward a state of being fully alive.

The key to consciously choosing lies in becoming aware of your habits then taking the inspired action needed to break the habits that don't serve you. Breaking habits is not easy. Some of our habits are rooted back to childhood. Others came on strong and have been with us ever since. We've formed habits around how we treat people, how we react when we're upset, drugs (yes, sugar and coffee are drugs), eating, and even relationships. Breaking habits takes dedication and effort. It's hard work.

Fortunately, there's an equation that states: work = reward.

The harder the work, the greater the reward.

So, which of your habits would you like to break?

What habits are not serving you and prevent you from living fully?

Some of you may immediately hear answers to these questions. For others, clear answers may be more elusive. Either way, you can benefit from increasing awareness around your habits.

Fortunately, there are strategies you can implement to develop increased awareness around your habits. Some of these strategies include:

- Using moments of beauty as triggers of awareness. Every time you see something that triggers the thought of beauty, do a sweep of your senses to take in the moment and appreciate the beauty that surrounds it.
- Use conscious decision making as a chance to step into your body and become completely aware. Decide to take some deep, conscious breaths, bringing your awareness inward. What do you want to do right now?
- Use emotions as a trigger of awareness. When you're feeling an emotion, acknowledge that you're feeling it. This is an opportunity to go into the body and feel what's there. Become aware of your emotion. Feeling is part of the human experience. Embrace it.
- When you're eating, and loving the food, use it as an opportunity to become fully present and aware. Experience the taste. Let the taste bring you into your awareness. Try eating alone in silence.
- Music can bring us into the body in a way that makes us fully present to the sounds we're hearing and the way those sounds are making us feel. Music is so powerful. Use it as a portal into presence where you're fully alive and aware.

- Make a practice of getting silent and still, and becoming fully aware. Feel into your senses. Try to carry this state with you into the hours that follow.

- Track the time between your periods of having complete awareness. When you start paying attention, you may notice that your periods of embodied self-awareness are days or maybe even weeks apart. As you place awareness on becoming aware of your moments of complete awareness, the time between moments of awareness will continue to shrink. The distance between these moments can continue to shrink until you exist in a place of continued awareness.

The point is that it doesn't matter what you do to gain awareness as long as you work toward gaining awareness. The objective of this practice is to move from a place of sleepwalk to one of conscious creation. From sleeping to *being*.

Habits can serve as a portal to *being*. Since we are naturally habitual beings, we can use our habits as an opportunity to take control of our lives.

The more awareness we have, the more control we gain. The more control we gain, the more freedom we experience. The more freedom we experience, the more beauty we see, the more enjoyment we have, and the more powerful we become.

It's all related.

And it all starts with awareness.

Habits are not limited to what you do or when you do it. You also have mental and emotional habits that can have just as big of an effect on your overall being as your physical habits.

Your mental habits affect your thoughts and general wellbeing. While most people have both positive and negative mental habits, like physical ones, your mental habits can be reformed. By developing awareness around your negative mental habits, you can see the negative impact they have on your life. This is generally enough motivation to inspire a plan to change them.

For example, let's say you develop awareness around your negative mental habit of dwelling on negative stories you hold about the past. With this new found awareness, you see the unnecessary stress and disharmony the dwelling has caused. You see how these negative stories have brought you down, caused frustration, and hurt relationships. In seeing these negative side effects, you are inspired to change this mental habit. You reflect on negative stories you're still holding of the past and work to rewrite them. Moving forward, when events unfold in a way that's less than ideal for you, you consciously write a positive story of the event in the present. You no longer allow yourself to hold onto negative stories.

You reprogram the old mental habit with a new one.

It's the same process for emotional habits.

In seeing how your negative mental and emotional habits are holding you back and preventing you from being fully alive, you can find the inspiration to change them. With this inspiration, you can take inspired action to replace the old negative habit with a positive new one.

It's also worth noting that it's almost impossible to upgrade habits you are unaware of. Subconscious mental habits will continue until you develop awareness around them. Like most aspects of self-improvement, growth begins with awareness.

To gain awareness around your mental habits, start paying attention to how you use your brain. What do you think about? Where do you dedicate your mental power? What does your mind do when someone's talking to you? When your mind wanders, where does it wander to? Is your mind thinking positive thoughts about the world around you or negative thoughts? Does it have a habit of seeing the positives or the negatives?

While the why behind each of these answers is complex, they are habits you have the ability to change. This said, it's much easier to change the habit when you understand the why behind it. Why do you see the negatives instead of the positives? Why do you get distracted so easily? Why do you think about the things you do?

The why behind things generally leads you to the root of its existence. At the why, you can see the origins from which the habit grew. When you cut it off at the roots, it's almost impossible for it to grow back.

So, how do you rip out the roots of a negative mental habit? I recommend beginning with a plan for how you'd like to upgrade the mental habit. How do you want to change your mental habit? There's a common belief among psychologists that the easiest way to change an existing habit is to replace it with a new one. If the negative mental habit is seeing things as limited, you can change it to seeing the abundance. Create a list of all the ways you see limitations: finances, love, time, etc. Then, after creating a list of all your mental habits around limitations, re-write them with an abundant perspective. You can then partner this list with the awareness you've developed around that mental habit to catch it when it occurs and rewrite it.

This is an example of changing a mental habit around a thought or belief.

But you can also change mental habits in regard to how you use your mind.

Science is now proving the benefits of positive mental habits on your emotions, intelligence, and skills. Adding new, positive mental habits can help you feel better, improve your intelligence, and make you more skilled.

Some of the most proven positive mental habits include:

- Practicing gratitude
  - List 5 things you are grateful for at the end of each day. This practice supports you in experiencing more gratitude on a moment-to-moment basis.
- Checking in with yourself
  - This is more of a weekly or monthly habit than a daily habit. I do it with the new moon and full moon. My check-in consists of asking myself what

I'm feeling, what's coming up for me, where am I thriving, and where am I struggling? What have I succeeded with? What are my intentions for the upcoming cycle? After asking myself each question, I sit in silence to observe the answer. This habit facilitates self-reflection and personal growth.

- Growth mindset
  - Creating a habit around growth and development can help you improve in all areas of life. Before bed, you can reflect upon where you could have improved today. What could have you done better? How could have you shown up more? This practice helps facilitate a growth mindset where you are continually looking for opportunities to learn and grow.
- Journaling/writing
  - Journaling provides your mind a place to release its thoughts, getting them out of the mind and down on paper. Journaling has been shown to decrease stress, facilitate learning from past experiences, and increase meaning, purpose, gratitude, and self-esteem.
- Mindfulness/meditation
  - Meditation is beneficial in so many ways. It can be argued that meditation is the most beneficial mental habit you can create. Pick a time and make it happen.

I've created a nighttime routine that incorporates gratitude practice, the growth mindset, and meditation. There are a few other aspects to my nighttime routine, but these are three pillars that facilitate positive, healthy habits. My moon routine includes a personal check-in and journaling. By creating time and space for these positive mental habits to occur, they are given an environment to flourish.

When you decide you want to add some new positive mental habits to your life, create the time and space for them and they will thrive.

Now that we've covered habits from a variety of perspectives, let's observe some of our most popular habits:

Coffee:

Caffeine is a drug. Drugs affect our bodies. There is a basic universal law that states what goes up must go down. Coffee brings us up. Which in turn brings us down.

While living on a yo-yo is an option that many choose, it may not be the most effective path. These ups and downs can take a toll on our bodies. They can lead to dependency and addiction.

One aspect to achieving complete freedom is developing freedom of dependency and addiction. Although we live in a society that has normalized -and even honored- coffee, it isn't necessarily the best thing for us.

Like everything, coffee carries a vibration. There is an energy associated with coffee that can be rather intense. While it's an energy that can be used as a powerful tool, it can easily become a hindrance. It is not an energy of calmed focus. It is not an energy of zen bliss nor one of loving presence.

Like all drugs, coffee can be used as a tool rather than a dependency.

The energy behind tea is very different from that of coffee. Green Tea carries more of the focused calm, zen bliss, and loving presence. Black tea lies somewhere between green tea and coffee.

Again, tea should also be used as a tool as opposed to a necessity. When we consciously consume coffee from a place of awareness, it can be an incredibly powerful drug. But, when we unconsciously consume caffeine, it can become problematic.

Alcohol:

Alcohol is another major drug that we have normalized in today's world. There was a meme going around online stating that alcohol is the only drug we have to explain not using.

Alcohol has become more normalized than milk.

Yet, just because we normalize something doesn't mean it's healthy. TV is still the norm in most American homes. But it's not healthy. The same can be said for sugar. Just because we've normalized it doesn't mean it's healthy. Alcohol is similar.

Alcohol has been accepted as one of our primary tools for dealing with daily struggles or social difficulties. We use it to relax and to have fun. It can enhance celebrations and often taste like a sweet nectar of fermented goodness.

While alcohol does have a positive side, it also carries a variety of downsides.

Alcohol is not of the highest vibration. In general, alcohol carries a low vibration of unaligned discourse. It doesn't put you in alignment with your highest self like medicines of the Earth may. Rather, it may do the opposite as it can detach us from our feelings and separate us from source. It can make us tired, irrational, emotional, lazy, aggressive, and unhealthy.

Alcohol often leaves us feeling like crap.

At the same time, we can remember that there is beauty in moderation. Alcohol pairs well with celebration as it can enhance our environment and make it all even more fun. It can pair well with a beautiful day in the sun and hits the spot after a long day of yard work.

But like all drugs, it's more effective when consumed consciously. Having a drink or two during special celebrations can enhance the celebration.

Alcohol can be a tool to help you be more fully alive in the present.

The key is consciously consuming a healthy amount of alcohol for your individual being. This is different for everyone. Some people have toxic relationships with alcohol and should not consume it at all. Others have symbiotic relationships with alcohol that help them be more fully alive. Like most things, it's about knowing yourself and your path.

When it's time for you to cut back (or cut out) alcohol, you will know… as long as you're listening and are aware of your body. Your body knows what serves it and what doesn't. Listen.

Consuming a few conscious drinks in the proper setting has a very different energetic frequency than putting down 6 alone in your living room. 6 is not healthy. Yet, we've normalized it as part of our American society.

Part of our work is in learning what works for us. It's not learning what works for society as a whole and playing along with that narrative, but learning what works for us as individuals. We are all so different. It doesn't really matter what works for someone else, we need to find what works for us. And that takes effort.

There are a few last aspects of alcohol I'd like to touch on. The first being that while I said alcohol can enhance the environment and help us be more fully alive in the present, it can also do the opposite. Alcohol can add a blurred lens to our environment and detach us from truly feeling the energy that's present. It can remove us from our environment just as much as it can connect us.

If we want to connect deeper to ourselves and the world around us, Alcohol is not the ideal substance. Ideally, if we're looking to connect, we do so from a sober place of centered alignment. This is arguably the most effective place to connect from. There are some plant medicines that can be incredibly powerful crutches to help us open and align ourselves with the present in a way that supports us in connecting deeply, but ideally, we get to the place of being here always so we can make these deep connections to others and our environment on a continual basis.

As I said above, there's a time and place for alcohol. I don't shun it like many in the spiritual community. Like everything on our planet, it serves a purpose. And, like everything, it needs to be used with reverence and respect. When we develop our relationship with alcohol to a harmonized place of healthy balance, we can partake in this Earthly pleasure in a productive way that's aligned with our higher self, rather than consuming it in a hurtful way that brings discord and disarray.

Cannabis:

Cannabis can be one of the Earth's great treasures. It can also be one of our greatest distractors. Like most items on this list, it's your relationship with cannabis that is so important.

When used consciously, cannabis can connect us to the vibration of the planet. We can feel a greater connection with the environment around us and see ourselves more clearly. It can elevate our thoughts and creativity and support us in seeing through a new perspective.

At the same time, when cannabis is abused or we become dependent upon it, it can separate us from the reality of the world we live in. It can be used to deny or suppress emotions that want to be felt. It can be used to escape from the heaviness of the physical world.

When cannabis is used in a way that distracts or separates us from the realities of our world, it becomes majorly problematic. In this form, it detaches us from emotions and experiences that our body needs to feel. When we hide these emotions with cannabis, they are not integrated. They are suppressed, and will continue to flair up in discordant ways until we take the time to sit with these emotions and integrate them.

Like so much of this list, it's the relationship with cannabis that matters. If you use cannabis, your work is in learning to use it as a conscious enhancer of reality that supports you in going deeper into your world within and without, rather than a distractant that separates you from your inner and outer realms.

TV and technology:

Downtime is a necessity. We need to reflect and decompress in order to integrate and align. We can't keep charging forward without recharging our batteries.

However, some forms of downtime are more effective chargers than others.

Spending a few hours at night detaching and unwinding has become a staple of our modern society. While this time is supplemented with alcohol for many, others simply rely on television and technology.

There's a time and place for television as it's one of the most powerful mediums we have to showcase the natural. Movies can take the viewer into alternative realities that expand and challenge their thoughts. They can support us in feeling emotions and questioning reality. They can be lighthearted and fun. They can feel good. Again, we need downtime.

The question is whether spending your two hours of downtime each night watching television is the best use of your time. If you consciously make the decision that tonight, your brain and body are spent and you just need to zone out and relax, then tv might be the perfect tool. But suppose you habitually turn on the television the second you sit down to relax. In that case, you may want to examine this habit.

When we zone out with television, we detach from our current emotional state, suppress our mind, and detach from our body. Again, there is a time and place for this. However, for most of us, if we get real and honest with ourselves, we can acknowledge that detaching from our emotional state, suppressing our mind, and detaching from our body isn't what we need. It may be easy. And possibly even fun. But it's generally not in your highest good.

A nice upgrade to television can be reading a book or writing. If you're not ready for this step maybe transition by watching documentaries. Eventually, replace a night or two of television each week with reading or writing. Eventually, this can move to 5 or 6 nights a week of reading/writing and one or two nights of television.

Or, you can replace your nightly habit of television with a project you've been wanting to get into. Maybe something artistic and fun. Maybe you've wanted to learn an instrument or have a desire to create something. Maybe there's a passion project that's been calling you, but you haven't had the time to start moving toward it.

When you break the habit of nightly television, you gain the ability to consciously choose what you want to do on a nightly basis. This has become some of my most valued time as I'm generally in a quiet, uninterrupted space for me to connect with my highest self. Some nights that means I sit in front of the fire with my notebook, other nights, I'm playing music and celebrating the beautiful day I just experienced. Some nights are quiet and calm. Others are passionate and involved. It depends on the day I just had, the day I have coming up tomorrow, and what my being is needing at that time. Every once in a while, my need involves television. On these days, I'll watch an episode of Survivor or find a stimulating documentary on Mother Earth. It's rare, but there are days when I just need to shut it all down and be entertained. When this is what you need, and you're able to listen, receive, and act upon this need, rather than habitually watching on a nightly basis, television can shift from an unconscious habit that drains your life force to a valuable tool for relaxation and pleasure.

The other primary aspect of our technology habit is the internet and social media. The internet is arguably the most significant invention of the past 100 years. It's changed nearly every aspect of the world we live in, connecting people worldwide while radically increasing our access to information, encouraging new ideas and concepts to thrive, and a new planet to be created. Although many of us lived in the pre-internet world, it's hard to imagine the world without it.

Due to the monumental impact the internet has had on every aspect of our life and the ease and enjoyment it can provide, many people are turning to it for their downtime of disconnection and relaxation. If the internet is used intentionally, to research, learn, connect, share, work, or even enjoy, it can be an incredibly powerful tool. At the same time, if it's habitually used to disconnect from your body, distract your emotions, and suppress your thoughts, it can become an incredibly dangerous beast.

This is what social media has become for millions. It's a habitual scroll of detachment and disconnection.

When we use social media (or the internet) as a habitual distraction from the life in front of us, it can vampire our energy and emotions in a perpetual cycle of searching for one more dopamine hit. Social media can be dangerous. Like most things, if it's approached with awareness and intention, it can be meaningful and add benefit to our life. And, at the same time, if it's approached from a habitual state of detachment and distraction, it can become a detriment to our life.

Porn and Masturbation:

Although masturbation has been a thing for as long as we've had things to pleasure, our addiction to pornogrophy has run rampant with the growth of the internet.

Sex and sexuality are healthy.

But habitually jerking yourself off to low vibe images and videos of others is a drain on your life force energy. Your sexual energy is some of your most powerful life force.

Rather than continually releasing this energy to low vibrational images, you can hold, harness, and focus this energy toward living more fully alive. It can be inspiring, invigorating, and motivational when you focus on embracing your sexual energy and allowing it to build up within you (rather than releasing it). It's a life force energy that can be channeled into creating and manifesting.

At the same time, it can just as easily become an addiction that leaves you feeling drained in a state of wanting. It can warp your reality and desensitize your sexuality. It's not an effective use of time and is not a productive use of your life force energy. The more you can control your sexual energy, the freer you become.

Eating:

We all have habits around eating. Some people habitually eat from the time they wake up to the time they go to bed. Others habitually fast until mid-day, then eat as they want until 8 at night. It doesn't so much matter where you fall on this spectrum, as it does that you have awareness around your eating habits.

When we gain awareness of our eating habits, we can reflect upon these habits to decide if they are healthy habits or not. Which of your eating habits could be improved to make you healthier?

Simply putting awareness around eating helps improve your health as you become more aware of what you're putting in your body and how it makes you feel. You become aware of when you're eating out of habit and when you're eating out of hunger.

Morning / Night ritual:

The morning and/or night ritual is becoming an increasingly popular habit that has purely positive effects on your life. This ritual can be individualized to meet your personal needs and desires, but the general concept is taking some time when you wake and/or before bed to get yourself centered and grounded.

In the morning, it generally includes setting an intention and embodying the being you want to be that day. This can take place through yoga, meditation, journaling, or over a cup of tea. Again, you make it work for you. I have one dear friend who turns a vision board into a puzzle about 4 times a year. He puts the puzzle together each morning and continues to be the person he wants to be.

A morning ritual is a way for you to start the day intentionally. This might be with yoga or meditation. It could include journaling or a walk in nature. You get to choose. How do you want to start your day?

Your morning habit sets the course for your day. Choose wisely.

The night ritual is a way to intentionally conclude your day. It can include reflection on the day that just occurred, a celebration of the day's successes, acknowledging where you could improve, setting intentions/goals/plans for the day to follow, yoga, meditation, or any other positive habit that serves you.

The morning and night rituals are examples of positive habits that can have a tremendous effect on your day-to-day living.

We have habits around each aspect of our day and each aspect of our life. The more awareness you develop around your habits, the more you move to a place of living in conscious presence. In this place, you are in the driver's seat of your reality. You choose what you do and how you respond rather than unconsciously reacting to the environment around you.

Your habits can serve as a trailhead to major growth. You can create positive habits that have beautiful effects on your life, and you can use negative habits to practice presence and awareness.

Your habits can help you or hurt you. They can serve you or suppress you. Again, choose wisely.

Chapter 12 Summary

Recap:

- Research has found that about 90% of what people do on any given day is habitual.
- The more conscious decisions you make, the fewer habits you follow.
- List and record your habits. Become aware of them. Transform the habits that do not serve you.
- Your mental and emotional habits have as big of an effect on you as your physical habits.
- Implement positive mental habits to help yourself live fully alive.

Questions to consider:

- Which of your habits have a negative effect on your life? Which has a positive effect?
- What is a positive habit you'd like to form that you have not yet? How can you form it?

- What are your most prominent mental habits? What are your emotional habits?

Challenge:

- Schedule "unscheduled" time for you to consciously choose what to do. Pick a few chunks of time a week that you block off for you to consciously choose what to do. When this time comes, sit with yourself. Check in. What are you being called to? What is most appealing. What will most serve you and make you feel most alive? Upon finding answers to these questions, do it. When you're done, reflect. How did it feel to consciously choose what you wanted to do? How did this serve you? How can you do more of this?

Being in Control vs Surrender

Release control and surrender to be.

"Freedom is the only worthy goal in life. It is won by disregarding things that lie beyond our control."

-Epictetus, Greek stoic philosopher

"Always say "yes" to the present moment. What could be more futile, more insane, than to create inner resistance to what already is? What could be more insane than to oppose life itself, which is now and always now? Surrender to what is. Say "yes" to life - and see how life suddenly starts working for you rather than against you."

-Eckhart Tolle, German born spiritual teacher and self-help author

"What is the surrendered state? It means to be free of negative feelings in a given area so that creativity and spontaneity can manifest without opposition or the interference of inner conflicts.

To be free of inner conflict and expectations is to give others in our life the greatest freedom. It allows us to experience the basic nature of the universe, which, it will be discovered, is to manifest the greatest good possible in a situation. This may sound philosophical, but, when done, it is experientially true."

-David R. Hawkins, American psychiatrist, physician, researcher, and spiritual teacher

As a human being, you have control over much of your personal environment. You are a powerful creator who designs your environment through the thoughts you hold, the words you speak, and the actions you make. You are energy, and your thoughts and actions are energy in return.

The energies you put into the world combine with the collective energies around you to create the environment you exist within.

You also have control over where you live, what you do, how you do it, and who you do it with. You exist with the free will to choose so many aspects of your life. Ultimately, you are the creator of your reality.

Unfortunately, many people never own the fact that they have this control. They continue to exist as human doings, running through the rat maze, never stepping into their power or taking ownership of their reality. Many people never awaken from their sleep to see the beauty and power of their true authentic being.

In return, they often feel a sense of the world being done to them instead of being created through them. This often creates the victim mentality that is so prevalent in today's world.

Taking control over that which you have control of is a choice. You choose your job. If you don't like it, choose a new one. You choose where you live. If your location doesn't serve you, choose a new location. You choose how you spend your time and who you spend it with. You have control over what you consume, how you spend your money, and what you do for fun. These are significant choices. Choose wisely.

When you consciously choose how you spend your time, you take some control of it. When you consciously choose who you surround yourself with, what you think, and what you consume, you regain control over your day-to-day existence.

This is a beautiful space to exist in. It's a space of autonomy and freedom of being.

However, in the freedom you have been granted, there's an element of surrender that's equally significant. Mother Earth has existed for almost 4.6 billions years. Nature is perfect exactly as is. The Universe is believed to be almost 14 billion years old. It's even older and wiser than Mother Earth. The Universe and Mother Earth understand the perfect balance between all that is. They control the laws upon which we have been created. For, within these laws, harmonized balance will remain.

Therefore, when you hold a thought or vision that is in alignment with the highest good of yourself and our planet, you will receive the guided empowerment to manifest it in reality. It may show itself with a different face than you intended and appear on a different timeline than you anticipated, but it will always appear in divine timing, in perfected form.

However, in order for you to manifest your reality, you must surrender to the perfection of the Universe and allow it to be. You must release your expectations, timeline, and egoic desires and allow the Universe to manifest your desire in its highest form.

You can set an intention for the outcome that is in alignment with your highest good, then release control as to how that outcome is created. Release the how, and surrender to the flow of creation. In this surrender, you can take inspired action to move toward the intention every day. Hold the vision as clear as light, and surrender any connotations you hold in regard to how the vision is achieved. Take inspired action daily with the tools, resources, and skills that you have. While doing so, remain open to all possibilities and options that arrive along the way. Use intuition to guide you. Sit in silence and hold your vision in high definition. Place yourself in the space of seeing the vision manifested. Feel the energy and excitement in that moment. Allow that feeling to embody you. Use that energy as a personal guide.

It's a beautiful dance between control and surrender as you are all-powerful yet hold no power. This balance is found in the place of *being*.

Life will always produce unexpected events. These events can shake your foundation and force you to re-imagine your future.

When you unexpectedly lose a loved one, your life changes. When someone who has always been in your life unexpectedly transitions, you need to re-calibrate.

The same re-calibration occurs when a long-term relationship ends. Relationships don't always work out as we plan. When this happens, a modified vision for the future becomes necessary.

What about your job? When you lose a job, your financial future can move to a place of uncertainty, leaving you in a place of stress and fear of what will come next.

When the image you hold for your future can no longer be obtained, you are left with uncertainty. You need to paint a new picture. A new foundation may need to be laid upon which you can move forward.

In each of these examples, there was an outside occurrence over which you had little to no control. If you try to force your desired reality upon the existing reality, you will be met with frustration and struggle. If, however, you surrender to the divine perfection of the Universe, and allow yourself to embrace its unknown and mysterious nature, you can remain in the flow, adapting, evolving, and enjoying as you go.

It's moving forward from a place of *being* rather than remaining in a place of doing. It's putting the oars up and enjoying the ride rather than sitting in the driver's seat, trying to go where you want.

Do you see the irony here? For most of the book, I've referenced taking the driver's seat and creating your reality rather than going along for the ride. Now, I state the opposite. It's the polarity and duality we exist within. There's always another side.

I spend a lot of time being the driver. I've created a vision and taken inspired action to manifest that vision. I've created a reality that I love living in.

There's power to driving. It has a time and place.

But the divine timing of the universe is out of our control. The more we hold to our vision for the way we want it to be, the harder the ride becomes. Swimming upstream is tough. Swimming in alignment with the flow of the current is a much easier swim. Granted, sometimes the salmon swim upstream. There's a time and a place to know what we need and take inspired action to create it.

It all exists within the balance of the universe. Holding intention for the lifestyle you view as your highest good, or the job most aligned with your passion and purpose is productive. When you hold a vision, you can take inspired action to create it. This is part of your power in human form.

But holding expectations as to how and when your vision unfolds is setting yourself up for failure. Some of it is just out of your control.

We have a limited vision of the reality we exist in. We have a fraction of the information. We don't understand all the factors at play and rarely see the true meaning behind it all. We don't really know what's best for us. Often, what we want is not what we need.

What you do have control over is the river you're floating in. Where are you living? Who's around you? How do you spend your time? You create the container.

You have control over the skills you are floating with and what you do while you're floating.

Do you have some survival skills and know how to swim? The more skills you enter the river with, the more prepared you are for whatever it throws at you. How skilled are you when you enter the water? Then, what do you choose to do when you're in there? Do you sink or swim? Go upstream or down? Do you choose the more exciting path or the safer one? Or, do you just float and allow the river to take you?

Most of the time, you'll move with the water smoothly, laughing and playing, doing as you choose, present in the flow. In these times, you can paddle along, taking action to move forward as you exercise your free will.

But sometimes, you'll face waterfalls. When the waterfalls come, you can try finding a rock to hold onto, but at some point, you need to surrender to the waterfall and go along for the ride. Put up the oars and release control. Have faith.

When you try holding onto the top of the waterfall, you'll find yourself stuck. You can temporarily hold yourself there, fighting the current, doing all you can to hang on. But eventually, you'll need to move forward. Sometimes, you need to have faith and take the leap. You need to surrender to the situation and allow it to flow naturally. In this flow, things generally work out as needed. Sure, it can be scary as all hell. It takes a lot of surrender and faith. But most of the time, this is exactly what you need.

Finding the place of surrender and faith allows you to be present and accept each moment as it appears rather than resisting it because it does not look the way you expected it to. It helps you to meet the moment neutrally, without judgment. From here, you can acknowledge its beauty, accept its reality, and continue along your journey.

However, it's worth noting that surrender is very different from apathy. With inspired surrender, you still hold intention and take action toward manifesting that reality. There is no room for apathy in manifesting your desired reality.

Rather, in surrendering, you detach from the journey's destination, and release control over how it's obtained. You still take inspired action to do your part to call it forth, but the details of where, when, and how are handed to the Universe.

In this place, you acknowledge that you can do all you can do, and you can do no more. The best you can do is your best. Your job is to show up every day with love and light, engage, and do your best. From this place of knowing that you're showing up and doing your part, you can then have peace for the form in which it unfolds… however far from your vision the reality may be.

At the same time, the more connected you become with your highest self, the more you integrate your energy and align with your being, the more similar your reality will look to your vision. It's all connected.

When building and launching SOUL Charter School, I had an inspired vision as to what a revolutionary model of education needed to look like. When I was introduced to my co-founder, Marissa, our visions were almost identical. But there were some differences. We had to release some of the control we held over our visions and allow these visions to merge.

We then held beliefs and desires over the timeline for opening the school, the location of the school, and the budget. With each of these aspects of SOUL, we continually took inspired action toward manifesting them with our ideal in mind while still holding space for them to unfold in their own perfected ways. We had to release our vision and surrender to the vision of the Universe.

It's similar to finding and pursuing your eco niche. When you hold a tight vision of what you want to do and how you want to serve, you might not be open to seeing how the Universe wants you to serve. You can take inspired action to move toward creating your dream job, but you need to hold space for it to be shaped and inspired by what the world needs.

The same can be said for many people's experience when entering into sacred plant ceremonies. They hold intention for what they want to get out of the ceremony or what they want to work on, but the plant medicine will give you what you need, rather than what you want.

When the path the plant wants to bring you down is met with resistance, the experience can turn negative. However, when we're open to receiving the plant's guidance and releasing control of our desire for the experience, we can move deeply into the depths we need to explore. While releasing control and surrendering to these experiences might initially be perceived as frightening, the light on the other end of the experience will be some of the brightest you've ever seen.

It's a delicate dance between control and surrender, but once you learn the moves, it becomes a freeing dance of unlimited possibility.

Chapter 13 Summary

Recap:

- You have free will to consciously choose most aspects of your life.
- Your reality is created through you.
- Set intention for the outcome you desire but surrender to how that outcome becomes reality.
- Sometimes, you hop in the driver's seat and take control. Other times, you put up the oars and enjoy the ride.
- There are some aspects of reality that are outside of your control. Surrender to the perfection of nature.

Questions to consider:

- How do you exercise your free will?
- Where can you take more control? How can you be more proactive in creating your desired reality?
- Where could you surrender more? What are you rejecting or struggling with that you could surrender to?

- What does it feel like when you're in control? What does it feel like when you're in surrender? What are your personal pros and cons to both control and surrender?

Challenge:

- Cold plunge. The cold plunge allows you to practice surrendering while simultaneously exercising control. Fill up your bath with cold water. Pour in a few bags of ice. Take control and get yourself in the water. Surrender to the temperature. Regulate your breathing. Surrender to the pain. Regulate your breathing. Try to stay in for at least 3 minutes. The more effectively you can regulate your body in the ice bath, the more effectively you can regulate it in other high-stress situations.

CHAPTER 14

Being Free

Freedom is a universal desire of all physical beings.
Find your freedom and fly.

"We must be free not because we claim freedom, but because we practice it."

-William Faulkner, American Writer

"Letting go gives us freedom, and freedom is the only condition for happiness. If, in our heart, we still cling to anything - anger, anxiety, or possessions - we cannot be free."

-Thich Nhat Hanh, Buddhist monk, and peace activist

"And the turtles, of course...all the turtles are free, as turtles and, maybe, all creatures should be."

-Dr. Seuss, American children's book author and illustrator

Living authentically, in alignment with your true calling and desires while embodying all aspects of your diversity, empowers you to exist in a place of being fully alive.

Unfortunately, our individuality has been suppressed to create a generic mass of generalized sameness. We have not been encouraged to create our own path and do our own thing. Instead, we're pushed down the same beaten path that our great grandparents paved, living an "easy life" as we accept the norm at face value.

This is a path that does not encourage you to think critically or question why things are the way they are. It's a path of college degrees, 40-hour-a-week jobs, 2.5 kids, divorce, 40 years of work, and daily medication. This path encourages television at night, drinking on the weekend, and voting for a Republicrat every 4 years. It creates a lifestyle based on buying things to justify our exhausting and draining working hours. It's a lifestyle that hands control over to the powers that be, so we can mindlessly drift through existence in a sleeping state of ignorant comfort.

As John F. Kennedy stated, "Conformity is the jailer of freedom and the enemy of growth." Conformity is not a path of freed autonomy, self-exploration, independent thought, or personal sovereignty. It's not a path of growth.

In order to truly be, we need freedom, autonomy, self-exploration, independent thought, and personal sovereignty. Fortunately, these are natural human rights granted to most humans on the planet. We have the power to accept these freedoms and step into our sovereignty. This is a choice that can be made by any person, at any time, of any day.

When you've finally had enough of the status quo and are ready to emancipate yourself from the matrix, you can. This is a choice you can make. You can choose which path you want to walk, the path of the masses, or your own individualized one. You choose how deeply you explore the depths of your shadow, how thoroughly you think, and how much inspired action you take to create your reality. When you are ready to awaken from the sleepwalk, you can claim your independence.

But it will change everything.

Maybe not overnight, but eventually, everything will change. You will question your job and who you are. You will challenge the beliefs you were fed and develop new ones that are homemade. You will develop a new understanding of who you are and who you want to be. You will find a new perspective on why you do what you do and how you exist within the world around you. You'll lose friends and develop new ones. You'll probably leave your job. You'll start expressing yourself differently and will develop new interests.

Through the process, you'll acknowledge that you're alive with greater energy flowing through you than you ever remember. You'll uncover new talents and find new passions.

You'll remember who you truly are and experience a peace you've never before felt. It will become contagious. You'll continue to go deeper. Life will never be the same.

You will begin to *be*.

You will be alive. You will be real. You'll be passionate, caring, educated, aligned, powerful, peaceful, and happy. You will be you… the greatest thing there is to be.

This freedom to be fully yourself, living authentically, aligned with your passions -and ideally your purpose- is one of the greatest human pursuits.

Paving your own path can be scary, and, at times, it might be more work. It's not the beaten path that is commonly traveled. Walking the path paved by society is definitely easier. You can set a routine and put it on autopilot. This traditional path of sameness is safe and predictable. But it's not necessarily fulfilling. It doesn't give your soul the opportunity to experience and express itself the way it desires. It doesn't get the full human experience. And, it probably never finds its purpose. It doesn't fulfill its eco niche. Lessons and learnings are lost. Growth and development are stalled.

What's easy isn't generally what's best.

The individualized path of inspired creation that serves is where the beauty is at. This path leads to everything your soul's looking for. It fulfills in all ways.

In Robert Greene's book, *Mastery*, he explains the individualized path through a different lens that's still relevant. Greene states, "Whatever field of activity we are involved in, there is generally an accepted path to the top. It is a path that others followed, and because we are conformist creatures, most of us opt for this conventional route. But Masters have a strong inner guiding system and a high level of self-awareness. What has suited others in the past does not suit them, and they know that trying to fit into a conventional mold would only lead to a dampening of spirit, the reality they seek eluding them.

And so inevitably, these Masters, as they progress on their career paths, make a choice at a key moment in their lives: they decide to forge their own route, one that others will see as unconventional, but that suits their own spirit and rhythms and leads them closer to discovering the hidden truths of their objects of study. This key choice takes self-confidence and self-awareness–the X factor that is necessary for attaining mastery...”

That's one aspect of freedom. Freeing yourself from the factory model of existence to pursue your own path. Then, when you're on your path, there are additional aspects of freedom you can pursue to enhance and optimize the human experience. The most significant of these include emotional freedom, mental freedom, physical freedom, and spiritual freedom. Once these four aspects of freedom have been found, financial freedom can come into play. However, without these four aspects of freedom solidified, financial freedom remains rather irrelevant.

Emotional freedom is integrating your emotions to harmoniously align their energy. With emotional freedom, you hold no grudges, resentment, animosity, anger, frustration, or judgment. You're not holding any weight from the past. With emotional freedom, you are light and pleasant. You're open and clear. As we discussed earlier, integrating the energy of your major life events takes some work, but it's some of the best work there is to do. It's the work that leads to emotional freedom.

Mentally you can find freedom by developing conscious awareness of your mind. With *mental freedom*, you can catch your negative thoughts and re-write your negative stories to foster a mind that serves you. You are not meant to serve your mind. It's an incredible tool for which we're blessed, but it is not our master. To develop mental freedom is to create a relationship where your mind is free to think and explore ideas and concepts, daily doings, and the wonder of existence. And, as it does what it does, you maintain the ability to focus it, shift it, expand it, and use it in the ways that best serve you. Then, if it tries to create a thought or idea that doesn't serve you, you have the power to check in with yourself and see if this idea or thought resonates. Is it legit? Is it a real thing, or is it a story your mind is creating? This discernment is the path to mental freedom.

Physical freedom is having the health and fitness to pursue the full human experience. With physical freedom, you're not affected by physical limitations. You can hike the trail, play in the water, dance to the music, play with the kids, and use the physical body. Physical freedom might not be as impactful as mental and emotional freedom, but it's still an aspect of freedom that affects your ability to be fully alive.

Spiritual freedom is almost a combination of all the other forms of freedom, putting your soul in a place where it's free to pursue its spiritual growth. When you're stuck in mental slavery or emotional fog, it's hard to open yourself to expand spiritually. Spiritual freedom is a place of open-minded exploration of consciousness and love. Spiritual freedom is a passion-driven pursuit of purpose with a commitment to ongoing growth. It's an acceptance to not knowing while still pursuing connection to universal consciousness.

The last concrete form of freedom to touch on is *financial freedom* and the freedom of possessions. This begins with a shift in perspective from valuing the man-made aspects of society to valuing the unseen wonders of an etheric nature. Society teaches us to prioritize accumulation of wealth for material possessions. These material possessions are believed to make life easier and more enjoyable when in reality, they distract us from the things that matter most. As you embody the concept of detachment, you acknowledge that material possessions don't matter nearly as much as you thought they did. There are tools that make our work far more effective and efficient and other objects we utilize to maximize our human experience. There is a place for these possessions. But in general, physical possessions aren't that important. There might be family heirlooms that give us a connection to the lineage that came before us, but outside of these types of objects, most "things" aren't really that important. We don't need to work half our life to accumulate things. Freeing yourself from this belief will free you in so many ways.

From here, you can step into the power of accepting that you have all you need.

We are born free, and we die free. May we find freedom in between.

This is a concept the Native Americans embodied as they lived simple lives, free of possession or 9-5 jobs. They lived freely with the land. In doing so, they observed the land and learned from it.

Chief Luther Standing Bear, a Lacota Chief in the early 1900s, said, "The animals had rights - the right of man's protection, the right to live, the right to multiply, the right to freedom, and the right to man's indebtedness. This concept of life and its relations filled us with the joy and mystery of living; it gave us reverence for all life; it made a place for all things in the scheme of existence with equal importance to all."

In observing the freedom and natural rights of animals, he acknowledged that there's an "equal importance to all." Animals are as important as humans, and the freedom of animals is as important as the freedom of humans.

While we no longer live in a society that prioritizes individual freedom, this freedom is still a foundational aspect of being human. Just as it is for the animals.

The Cherokee used the metaphor of directions to explain the priority they placed on the individual: North, South, East, West, Up, Down, and Where You Are. The final position of Where You Are places the individual at the center of their universe with the other directions all dependent upon where they stand. This perspective honors the importance of the individual as the star in their universe while implying that they hold the power to keep the universe balanced.

The Cherokees, Iroquois, and other Native American tribes saw the balancing of the universe as a product of lifelong self-discovery. In return, they supported artistic, sexual, philosophical, and spiritual experimentation. They allowed children to change their names as they saw fit. They encouraged the individual to define and redefine themselves throughout the course of their life. They were free to explore themselves and live authentically.

Ironically, America was built on similar principles, "life, liberty, and the pursuit of happiness." Liberty is defined as the state or quality of being free. The Declaration of Independence states that we as humans have these natural rights.

It's now time for us to reclaim these natural birthrights. You can pursue the life you want to live, find the liberty you desire, and experience happiness on a continual basis. These pursuits are your right. You must simply make the choice to embody these rights and pursue your freedom, as freedom is a pillar of living more fully alive.

Pursue freedom and live fully alive.

Chapter 14 Summary

Recap:

- You choose which path you walk. The traditional path might be easier, but it's not nearly as rewarding as a personalized path.
- Unplugging from the matrix is a powerful form of freedom.
- Integrate the energy of your past, and have peace with the present to find emotional freedom.

- You do not serve your mind. Free yourself from it.
- Freedom is a path to living fully alive.

Questions to consider:

- Do you follow the masses or pave your own path?
- What do you need to integrate in order to feel emotionally free?
- Where do you limit or restrict yourself?
- In what aspects of life do you experience the greatest freedom? Where are you most restricted and limited?

Challenge:

- Freedom night. I recommend you do it on a full moon, but any night will do. Give yourself a few hours to go outside, preferably in nature with some space, and allow yourself to be 100% free. Take your clothes off. Dance. Howl. Scream. Cry. Move your body. Feel it. Allow your energy to move. Freely. If you want to have a drink and enjoy a puff, then have a drink and enjoy a puff. If you feel like plant medicine, then hold a ceremony. Open yourself up and feel free. Shake and stretch. Sit in gratitude. Write. Think. Meditate. All with the intention of freedom. As the night concludes, reflect on your freedom. How free did you feel in this exercise? How free do you feel in your daily life?

Being Fully Alive

Embody your being and live fully alive.

"We are very good at preparing to live, but not very good at living. We know how to sacrifice ten years for a diploma, and we are willing to work very hard to get a job, a car, a house, and so on. But we have difficulty remembering that we are alive in the present moment, the only moment there is for us to be alive."

-Thich Nhat Hanh, Buddhist monk and peace activist

"If you want it, become it."

-Maston Kipp, American author, speaker, and life coach

"Life is a lovely process of becoming."

-Douglas MacArthur, American military leader

"To live is the rarest thing in the world. Most people exist, that is all."

-Oscar Wilde, Irish poet, and playwright

When we reflect back on how our ancient ancestors lived, we see their respect and reverence for life. They fought to survive. They withstood the elements and met their human needs through every disaster, disease, and difficulty they faced. They did all they could to continue living. And, when they succeeded in surviving another day, they would celebrate this triumph with gratitude and respect.

The reverence for life that was felt by our ancestors encouraged them to continue pushing on. They endured tough times. And they flourished in fun times. And, through all those times, they held a reverence for life that motivated them to keep pushing on. They kept moving forward. They survived, thrived, and evolved.

Their reverence for life has been passed down to us. It's within us.

However, with survival becoming as easy as it is today, this reverence for life doesn't come as naturally as it may have in our tribal times.

But this isn't an excuse to live apathetically.

There's nothing in life to be grateful for without life itself.

When reverence for life doesn't naturally appear, part of the work required is in developing that reverence. Experiencing reverence for life is a catalyst for living.

With reverence for life, you're motivated to live it.

When you see the beauty, wonder, and awe of life, you can't help but be a part of it. You grow motivated to be your part of it all. You become inspired to serve your eco niche. To be your full self.

As you find a reverence for life that motivates you to step into being your full self, you're living more fully alive.

For, what more could we possibly want out of life than living it fully? Is there any greater experience you could have than connecting with all aspects of yourself and supporting them to all thrive? Imagine your loving side being able to love, your creative side creating, your adventurous side exploring, your fun side playing, your intelligent side learning, your supportive side parenting, and your spiritual side connecting with source. When you create a lifestyle that allows all of your parts to be themselves and do the things you love to do, you become full. You are fulfilled. There is nothing more you could want.

The primary reason we want money is to find the freedom to do all the things we want to do. What if you could do them all today?

You already have the freedom to start creating the life you've always wanted to live! You can start creating it today.

What's holding you back?

We are complex and beautiful beings. To juice the nutrients out of life, sip its sweet nectar, and hit its biggest jackpots, we can't just thrive in one or two domains. Yes, we each have our strengths and areas we excel. We can get a lot out of life by maximizing our natural abilities and minimizing our weaknesses. This is a common approach in today's society.

Yet, while this philosophy may allow you to make good money and live comfortably, it's lacking holistically. You are so much more than your strengths and weaknesses. You are the sum of all you've ever thought, said, and done. You carry pieces of your ancestors, your biological family, and all the family you've developed along your journey. You are your work and your friends. Your hobbies and interests. Your trauma and demons. Your accomplishments and successes. You are a mental, emotional, physical, and spiritual body. You are so incredibly complex!

To maximize your human experience and suck all the marrow out of life, you need to find harmony within each of these parts of yourself. A chain will always break at its weakest link. You can only go as far as your weakest link will allow.

However, when you work back through each of your links to solidify their lessons and learnings, your steel is hardened. Your links strengthen, supporting you in going farther and living deeper. No link can be left weak if you are going to experience the outer edges of life and live fully alive.

You must find a job that serves you. Ideally, one that falls in your ikigai zone where your passions and strengths overlap with what the world needs and what you can be paid for. Better yet, is finding your eco niche, the specific role you came here to play.

This "job" then needs to blend with your hobbies, interests, and desires, to create a balanced lifestyle that allows you to pursue your passions and dedicate your time to your priorities.

In this place of holding a balanced lifestyle, you can start doing the work to improve all the other aspects of your being. You can make the changes and upgrades needed for your physical body to be healthy, your mental body to excel, your emotional body to feel peace, and your spiritual body to connect with your true self. You can do the work to improve your relationships with family and friends. You can go into your shadows and integrate your past. From here, you can rekindle your childlike self and bring play into your life. You can create positive habits and find that powerful balance between surrendering to the flow of life while taking inspired action to create your reality. You can reconnect with who you truly are and who you're meant to be. You can find freedom and experience bliss. You can live fully alive.

There's nothing greater you can do with your time here in physical form than make the most of it. Feel deeply. Love fully. Experience it all. Learn. Grow. Laugh and enjoy. Be.

These are pillars of the human experience. They are the foundation for your dream home. When these pieces all come together, a deeply grounded and unshakable foundation is established. On this rock-solid base, you have the ability to build whatever you'd like. You can confidently step out of your comfort zone to take some risks and explore new experiences. You can put yourself out there and pursue your passions. You can be who you've always dreamed of being.

I remember in my last year of college, I was substitute teaching during the day then coaching a Highschool baseball team in the afternoon. At night, I'd drive down to UAlbany for the last few classes of my master's degree. One of these final classes was the thesis. As the semester endured, I started to feel the weight of it all. It was a lot.

I let stuff build up and fell a bit behind. I tried to get on top of the work, but it just kept piling on. I was stretched thin and couldn't find the time for everything. The pressure built. It got the best of me. I would escape to the bars with friends on the weekends and wasn't as kind to my girlfriend.

I hadn't felt stress like that before then. I'd never felt that kind of pressure. It felt like there was weight hanging over me. I was shackled to the work I had to do. It weighed me down.

Then, as the semester started to wind down, the work slowed, and tasks were eventually completed. As they were completed, they lifted. When the thesis was complete, a major weight was lifted from me. I felt like I could start breathing again. Eventually, all the tasks were completed and the weight was gone. I felt as light as sunshine. I felt free.

I was on top of everything. There was nothing hanging over me. There were no shackles restricting me.

It was then that I acknowledged the power of being on top of life. When tasks come in, I get them done. I try to stay on top of things with nothing hanging over me.

This creates a freedom through which you can live fully alive.

When you have life tasks that need to be completed, an awareness of them exists within you. A piece of your bandwidth is tied to the task. Until that task is complete, this piece of bandwidth remains aware of the uncompleted task. Once it's complete, you're free from it. There is no longer any bandwidth tied to it.

With each task you complete, a shackle is cut. You become more free.

Eventually, you get to a place where there are no more ties. There is nothing holding you back or weighing you down. You can get on top of it all.

This is an empowering place to be. In this place, you are free to do what you choose.

Sure, more tasks will continually come in. Daily. Sometimes, multiple tasks a day. And, when you get them complete, you're again free.

Everything gets lighter. In this place, it's easier to laugh and smile. Play can re-emerge, and creativity can be inspired.

In this place, of being on top of life, you're being more fully alive.

However, staying on top of life isn't isolated to our physical to-do lists. It's equally important, if not more important, to stay on top of life from an emotional perspective. When you hold animosity and resentment for the past or stress and fear of the future, it's hard to be fully alive in the present. Being fully alive includes knowing what you're feeling and why you're feeling it. It's finding peace with the emotions of the past and holding trust in the future.

As Ram Dass said, "Be here now." There is no place you can be fully alive other than here in the now.

When you're on top of life, you can be here now. You can be fully alive in the present. When work is hanging over us needing to be completed, a piece of our presence is dedicated to ensuring that task eventually gets complete. This piece of your bandwidth will be tied to that task until it's completed.

This is the same with any other requirement that looms in your future or any emotion you carry from your past. A piece of your presence is tied to these aspects of the past or the future until they are finalized and resolved. It's extremely difficult to remain fully present in the now until you've cleared your past and your future.

But, once you do release everything in the past, and get on top of everything coming up in the future, you are truly free in the present. Being free in the present is an incredibly powerful and liberating place to be.

Being fully alive is as complex as it is individualized. It incorporates so many aspects of the human experience at large and so much of who you are personally.

Yet, when we boil it down to its essence, it's about enjoying yourself, feeling good, doing the things you want to do, contributing your part, and living aligned with your highest self. Being fully alive is loving yourself and those around you. And, it's loving

Mother Earth and the Great Spirit. For, through them, we are blessed with life.

And what a blessing life is.

When you live with a reverence for life and a passion for living, seeing the blessings that occur around you daily, the love for life becomes natural. From here, you can be fully alive.

Your job to get here is in doing the work. Integrate the emotions of your past. Find peace. Connect with your higher self and strive to align your life with this version of yourself. Improve your relationships. Balance your time. Pursue your passions. Envision your greatest life and take inspired action to manifest it. Take control of your life where you can. Surrender to that which lies outside of your control.

Then, have a lot of fun. Enjoy yourself. Laugh and play. Smile and laugh. Shine light. Be love.

Because although we don't know exactly why we're here, it's logical to conclude that part of the purpose is in enjoying the beautiful life we've been blessed to live.

If nothing else, you can at least strive to enjoy your life. Be kind and have fun.

And, maybe along the way, you'll gain some insight or read a book that inspires you to take it farther. Maybe you get motivated to step outside of your comfort zone and push the boundaries of the human experience. In doing so, you might experience a moment of being fully alive. Maybe, this feeling even becomes contagious, and you continue to step outside that comfort zone to expand yourself even further. Maybe you continue striving to live fully alive always.

Or, maybe you don't. Maybe you decide that you're good where you're at. So, you settle into a comfortable place and make the best of it.

There's no judgment either way.

But, if you want to be fully alive, you can't really live on repeat in a comfortable world of sameness. You have to keep evolving. You need to continue to challenge yourself, push your boundaries, take chances, and get uncomfortable. This is where you grow.

And, in this place of growth, you are being fully alive.

You are alive.

We might not know why we're here or what's the meaning of life, but we know that whoever is reading these words right now is alive.

And we know that as a human being, living on planet earth, you have free will. You get to choose what you do on a moment-to-moment basis.

We might not know what enlightenment is or exactly how to get there, but we do know that you can consciously choose how you live each moment of your life.

You get to choose what you do and how much you do it. And, you get to choose the energy you do it with. You choose how much work you do to improve and evolve yourself. You choose when you say yes and when you say no. You choose how fully you live.

We know that you can make the choice to take inspired action toward creating the reality you desire. We know you can create this reality.

It's all up to you. Do you choose to go into your triggers or run away from them? Do you go into your pain or suppress it? Do you feel your emotions, or do you numb them? Do you step out of your comfort zone to expand and grow, or do you remain stagnant within your zone of comfort?

These are choices for you to make. You have free will.

You choose whether you continue to carry weight from past experiences, or whether you use them as opportunities to learn and grow. And you choose whether you put life on autopilot and press repeat, or if you embrace its beauty to live fully alive.

Living fully alive is choosing to walk toward the life you dream of. It's being the greatest person you can envision yourself being.

It's contributing in the ways you can contribute, showing up with presence and awareness, and allowing your light to shine bright.

Living fully alive is doing all the things you've always wanted to do. And learning and growing from all of them. It's feeling your energy and emotions and channeling them into positives.

Being fully alive is singing and dancing, celebrating and connecting. It's getting beneath the surface to explore the depths of life. It's being wild and vulnerable. Open and engaged. It's letting your inner child out to play, your feminine in to nurture, your masculine in to do, and your higher self in to guide. It's pushing yourself to be your best, having fun, and enjoying your journey.

Being fully alive is connecting with your true authentic self. It's allowing your gifts and strengths to shine while pursuing your passions and interests.

Living fully alive is being there for yourself and those around you.

It's being present and aware in each moment, allowing yourself to embrace the beauty of daily life. It's remaining conscious of the decisions you make, the thoughts you think, and the beliefs you hold. It's consciously aligning these decisions, thoughts, and beliefs with your highest self.

Being fully alive is stepping out of your comfort zone, into your growth zone, to allow yourself to grow and expand as you embrace new experiences, emotions, and opportunities. It's loving that you're human and taking on as much of the human experience as you're capable of.

When you embrace all these aspects of yourself and your life on this planet, you support yourself in living fully alive. You allow yourself to shine. You can show up in the ways you want to show up and become the person you want to become. You can live the life you want to live.

Getting to this place of living fully alive is a choice you can make.

You choose to go within and integrate your past to use it as opportunities for growth. You choose to pursue your passions, do what you love, and say yes to the world when it presents you with new opportunities and experiences. You choose your perspective and the emotional state you're in. You choose how you live your life.

By choosing to live fully alive, all options are opened, new opportunities are presented, and higher vibrational states are obtainable. This choice allows you to take the driver's seat of life and control what you can control while surrendering to that which you can not. It's an empowering place of unlimited possibility. The Serenity Prayer summarizes this beautifully as it states, "God grant me the serenity to accept the things I cannot change, courage to change the things I can, and wisdom to know the difference."

This book serves as a guide to help you make this choice. It presented you with questions to consider, ancient wisdom to reflect upon, and philosophies to ponder. In reading through these pages, I hope they inspired you to consciously make the choice to pursue living fully alive.

Once this choice is made, it's up to you to do the work needed to integrate your past and show up aware in the present. Once the choice is made, the work begins. This is where the real beauty lies.

Find the pleasure in doing this work as it's arguably the most important work there is to do. Enjoy the journey. Embrace it all. Allow it to inspire and uplift you. Watch yourself grow and evolve. Celebrate the work you put in and the wins you experience. Smile at your successes as they fill you with light. Let this light shine bright.

You are a beautiful being full of unlimited possibilities. Step into your being, and live fully alive.

Chapter 15 Summary:

Recap:

- Reverence for life leads to an inspiration to live fully alive.
- Overfill yourself with self-love and allow it to overflow onto others.

- We can uplift humanity by being in service and support of others.
- There is no place you can be fully alive other than the here and now.
- When you let your light shine bright, it encourages others to let their light shine.
- Living fully alive is a choice you can make.

Questions to Consider:

- When do you most feel a reverence for life? How can you feel more of it?
- What do *you* need to fill yourself with self-love?
- How/where can you step more into your growth zone?
- Do you choose to live fully alive?

Challenge:

- Do something new every day this week. For the next 7 days, push yourself to have a new experience every day. Step outside of your comfort zone. Reflect upon how fully alive you felt during these experiences. Which of them made you feel most fully alive? Why did it make you feel so alive? What else can you do to make yourself feel this fully alive?

Closing Thoughts

"Whatever you are not changing you are choosing."
-Laurie Buchanan, American writer

There is no greater gift that we've been blessed with than the gift of life. Life's incredible. In every way.

At the same time, there are varying degrees of amazingness in which you can live. You have the choice of putting it in cruise control and coasting to the finish or fully engaging and driving where you dream of. When you choose to go within and do the personal work to release that which holds you back, integrate that which is unintegrated, and align with your highest self, you are given the opportunity to experience more of the entirety of the human experience. When you do the work, you're rewarded with the gift of living a truly amazing life.

In this place of living fully alive, life becomes overwhelmingly beautiful.

Sure, there are still challenges. Few of us have done all of our work and are living fully aligned with our highest self in all ways, always. There's still work to do.

Fortunately, we're now understanding the personal growth aspects of the human experience in new ways. We have an abundance of tools and techniques to apply and a variety of modalities to explore. There's support out there for everyone. No matter where you are on your personal journey, what it is you're working on, or how you want to do the work, there are strategies and supports available for you. Use them.

Hopefully, this book shone some light on aspects of your *being* that can be integrated and upgraded to become more fully alive. Hopefully, some of the modalities and techniques I shared resonate with you and can be of service. And, hopefully, some of the experiences and insights I've shared sparked some motivation and inspiration in you that can serve as support on your journey.

Because life can be challenging. We all have our share of struggles and personal work to do. Yet, the more tools we have to draw upon, the easier it all becomes. It doesn't need to be challenging. You don't need to remain in pain or discord. You have the ability to free yourself from all limited thoughts, negative beliefs, or fears that interfere with you living fully. This is why we do the work. To free ourselves from the limitations of our earthly experience so that we can live fully alive.

Then, hopefully, that which supported us on our individual journeys can support others on theirs. As we learn, we can pass it forward. For, the more we support each other, the more we can progress as a whole. As we do the work to grow and evolve individually, we grow and evolve as humanity.

When you live fully alive, in alignment with your highest self, you have the opportunity to fill your cup with self-love. You can see your gifts and abilities. You see what makes you different from others. You see your quirks and idiosyncrasies. And you see your beauty. You see where you show up and the effort you make. You see the work you've done and the work you still have to do.

As your cup is filled, you can allow it to overflow into the cups of others.

Flash extra smiles of sincere joy and happiness. Be quick to laugh. Speak words of kindness and encouragement. In doing so, you allow your light to shine bright, helping to light the way for others.

When you're in service and support of others, you're not only helping to raise them up, you are also helping to raise yourself. It's mutually beneficial. In this way, we can uplift humanity by being in service and support of others.

Listen to others and share wisdom and insight when asked. Lend a hand. Empathize. Give big happy hugs. Work with kids, the elderly, or the disabled. Serve the underserved. Contribute where you can.

Embracing the service aspect of living fully alive allows your positive energy to uplift, inspire, and support others. And, it allows the positive energy of those interactions and experiences to uplift, inspire, and support you.

Together we rise.

We live in an intense and wild time.

Our understanding of the cosmos is growing daily, yet as a society, we are failing to apply and adapt to all that we learn. It's not being applied at the top, making it impossible to trickle down through the masses.

Therefore, it must be applied from the ground up.

We, the people, have the power to change how we live.

You can consciously choose how you play your game of life. You can coast through it comfortably in a stabilized state of sameness, or you can stretch your boundaries in pursuit of new experiences and opportunities for growth.

It's your choice. You choose the lens through which you view your game.

Do you view it as an infinite game with the goal of continuing to play or a finite game where you coast to the finish?

We do not know for sure if we will come back to play again. But if you do, why not learn, experience, and grow as much as possible in this life, to come back with a leveled-up avatar next time around? And, if you do not come back, why not squeeze every last ounce out of the life you are blessed to be living right now?!

Either way you look at it, the choice is living. Living fully alive.

For, when you make the choice to consciously live your life fully alive, you become a beacon of light for others. You become the change.

We become the change.

It feels like the only way things will change is by us changing the way we live. When we live for the collective good of we, rather than the egoic pursuit of me, we raise and support each other to a higher state of being.

We can each do our part individually to shine our own light.

When you shine your light, it encourages others to shine their light.

As we all begin to shine, the Earth will illuminate.

Life feels like a blessed miracle that deserves our utmost reverence and respect. It gives me a profound love for Mother Earth and Humanity.

When we find this reverence for life, we are given the inspiration to embrace life fully. Often, this leads to a motivation to do our part to support the growth, development, and evolution of our people and our planet.

We've come so far and have created so much beauty in the world. And, we still have so far to go. In so many ways.

While we can't necessarily change the way our world "leaders" are harming the world around us, we can change our world within.

As more of us change the world within, the world without will naturally follow.

It feels like the greatest thing we can do for our planet and our people is to do our own personal work. Heal your pains and traumas, so you cause no more harm on any human ever. Then, maybe stop hurting animals. And the planet.

Be the change. Literally. In all aspects of life. Live the way you would idealize humanity living. And not just in the aspects of life that are convenient for you. If there are systems you don't believe in, stop supporting them. Use your dollar to support the businesses that are aligned with your morals and values. Align your life with the highest vibrational lifestyle you are capable of.

Often, this just means being love. Be love. Always. Just be love. There's no greater way to give thanks to Mother Earth than being loving to her and all the life she facilitates.

Finally, I want to give thanks to everyone who's doing the work. Everyone who's going within and integrating their past. Everyone who's bringing love and light into their world and shining it for others. Thank you to everyone who's being rather than doing, who's optimizing the human experience and living fully alive.

From my perspective, the universe has created itself to experience itself. Each of us are working our way back to a complete remembrance of who we truly are, where we come from, and why we're here. In our journey back to ourselves, we experience different aspects of the human experience. Together, with all other life, and each aspect of the universe, we experience it all. We get to live it. We get to be it. We are the universe. We are God. God is us. We all come from the same place. We all return to the same place.

By doing the work to be the person you are ultimately meant to be, you are bringing your ultimate gift to the world. Thank you.

Thank you for caring. And trying. Thank you for being you. Thank you for *being*.

About the Reader

You are a beautiful human being
full of love and light,
who's ready to shine even more bright.
You are growing and evolving,
appreciating your journey,
as you align with your authentic self
and live fully alive.

If you'd like to learn more about the reader
please continue to go within and do your self-work.
Show up in the world, pursue your passions,
spend time in nature, meditate, and reflect.

About the Author

Michael feels blessed to be alive.
He's obsessed with learning, growing,
and doing his work to shine more light.
He's passionate about supporting humanity
and does so through his extensive work in education,
the space he holds for his community,
and the words he puts on page.
His daughters are his greatest teachers and deepest loves.

If you'd like to get in touch or learn more
about his work please visit
www.michaeljgrimes.com

www.ingramcontent.com/pod-product-compliance
Lightning Source LLC
Chambersburg PA
CBHW051954150726
47999CB00004B/1379